JOURNEYING WITH LUKE
REFLECTIONS ON THE SUNDAY GOSPEL READINGS FOR YEAR C

Journeying
with Luke

*Reflections on the Sunday Gospel
Readings for Year C*

MARTIN HOGAN

VERITAS

Published 2018 by
Veritas Publications
7–8 Lower Abbey Street
Dublin 1
Ireland
publications@veritas.ie
www.veritas.ie

ISBN 978 1 84730 863 4

10 9 8 7 6 5 4 3 2 1

Extract on p. 35 is from 'A Christmas Childhood' by Patrick Kavanagh, from *Collected Poems*, edited by Antoinette Quinn (Allen Lane, 2004), by kind permission of the Trustees of the Estate of the late Katherine B. Kavanagh, through the Jonathan Williams Literary Agency.

Extract on p. 94 is from 'A Death in the Desert' by Robert Browning, from *Dramatis Personae*, London: Chapman and Hall, 1864.

A catalogue record for this book is available from the British Library.

Designed and typeset by Pádraig McCormack, Veritas
Printed in the Republic of Ireland by SPRINT-print Ltd, Dublin

Veritas books are printed on paper made from the wood pulp of managed forests. For every tree felled, at least one tree is planted, thereby renewing natural resources.

Contents

Introduction

During Year C, the Sunday Gospel readings are mostly taken from the Gospel of Luke. A great deal of Luke's Gospel will be read over these Sundays, sometimes entire chapters, and, at the very least, sections of each of the twenty-four chapters, apart from chapter eight. What kind of a Gospel did the evangelist Luke write?

The author of the Gospel we call 'Luke' was also the author of the Acts of the Apostles. He is the only evangelist to have written a work in two parts. He intended that they be read together. By the end of the second century, the two-volume work that we know as Luke-Acts was being attributed to Luke the companion of Paul (Phm 24; Col 4:14; 2 Tm 4:11). The 'we sections' in Acts (16:10–17; 20:5–15; 21:1–18; 27:1–28:16) may suggest that the author was a younger companion of Paul on some of his later missionary journeys. The author of this two-volume work is the only evangelist to speak of himself in the first person singular, 'I' (Lk 1:1–4). He is also the evangelist who shows the greatest interest in the history of the Roman Empire. He is careful to locate his story of Jesus and of the early Church in the context of that wider political world.

In the Gospels of Mark and Matthew, Jesus begins his public ministry by announcing that the kingdom of God is at hand. In Luke, however, Jesus begins his public ministry by going to his home synagogue in Nazareth and reading aloud from the prophet Isaiah (4:16–18). In Luke's Gospel, these verses from Isaiah are the first public words Jesus speaks after his Baptism. They serve as a programmatic statement for his ministry. The text of Isaiah that Jesus quotes is taken from 61:1–2, with a line drawn from 58:6. These two texts have one word in common, namely, 'release'. Jesus declares that 'today', the day of his ministry, is the time of 'release'. Such an announcement was, indeed, good news, especially for those who were in need of release.

The text from Isaiah 61 refers to the poor, the captives and the blind. The 'poor' were the economically impoverished. The 'captives' would have overlapped with the 'poor', many of whom were held captive by debt or in prison. Luke may also have understood the 'captive' as people who suffered from physical illness. He sometimes portrays the healing work of Jesus in terms of bringing release to the captive. In describing how Jesus healed Simon Peter's mother-in-law, the evangelist comments that Jesus 'rebuked the fever, and it *released* her; and immediately she rose and served them' (4:39; cf. 13:10–17). The text from Isaiah 61 also refers to the 'blind'. They represent all who suffered from physical disabilities. The text from Isaiah 58 makes reference to the 'oppressed'. In that passage the 'oppressed' are those who have been denied God's justice. These groupings all lived on the margins of the community.

The remainder of Luke-Acts would suggest that the terms 'poor', 'captive', 'blind' and 'oppressed' also refer to those who were marginalised because of what was perceived to be their sinful way of life. The Greek word that is translated as 'release' in Luke 4:18–19 refers to 'forgiveness' elsewhere in the Gospel of Luke; for example, 'Forgiveness [release] of sins is to be proclaimed in his name to all nations, beginning from Jerusalem' (Lk 24:47). Jesus gives 'release' by bringing God's forgiveness to those labelled 'sinners'. The 'blind', in that sense, are also the spiritually blind. Those regarded as 'sinners' are often referred to in Luke as the 'lost'. Jesus' ministry of release embraced all those who lived on the edge, whether for reasons of economic impoverishment, physical illness, or chosen lifestyle. Luke portrays Jesus going to those who are outsiders and bringing them the hospitality of God, releasing them from their state of exclusion, be it self-imposed or otherwise. This is how God visits his people. These opening words of Jesus' public ministry in Luke set the tone for the whole of his ministry which portrays him as reaching out towards the poor, the disabled, sinners, tax collectors, lepers, Samaritans, all who were considered outsiders for one reason or another, and bringing them God's hospitality, thereby reversing their lowly status. A great reversal is central to Luke's narrative (cf. Lk 1:51–3).

For Luke, this is what it means to say, 'the kingdom of God is at hand'. God's kingdom comes when those on the margins become full members of the God's people. At the end of chapter four, Jesus declares, 'I *must* proclaim the good news of the kingdom of God to the other cities also; for I was sent for this purpose' (4:43). This saying has a number of elements in common with the passage which Jesus quoted from Isaiah towards the beginning of that chapter: 'to proclaim'; 'to send'; 'good news'. The 'good news' mentioned in the text of Isaiah is now identified as 'the good news of the kingdom of God'. Whenever we read in Luke's Gospel that Jesus or his disciples were 'proclaiming the good news of the kingdom of God' (8:1), we have to think back to Luke 4:16–18 to fill out the meaning of that expression. God's kingdom comes when the excluded are included, when outsiders experience God's lavish hospitality, when those who are regarded by others as dishonourable are shown honour.

Jesus' quotation from Isaiah concludes with a reference to 'the acceptable year of the Lord'. The ministry of Jesus reveals a God who accepts people, especially those usually deprived of human acceptance. Luke highlights the irony that the one who embodied God's accepting, hospitable presence was not himself acceptable to the people of Nazareth, 'Truly, I say to you, no prophet is acceptable in his own country' (4:24). Initially, the people of Nazareth welcomed Jesus' gracious words (4:22). Why did the people of Nazareth go on to reject the one who announced the acceptable year of the Lord? They saw Jesus as belonging to them in a special way. 'Is not this Joseph's son?' they asked (4:22). As one of themselves, they expected him to show God's favour to them in a special way, 'Do here in your hometown the things that we have heard you did at Capernaum' (4:23). Jesus firmly resisted this pressure to show the people of Nazareth greater favour than others. Indeed, Jesus goes on to identify himself with two prophets of Israel who ministered, not only beyond Nazareth, but beyond Israel. Elijah and Elisha ministered to two Gentiles, a poor widow of Sidon, a Phoenician city, and a wealthy Syrian commander. The people of Nazareth were scandalised by Jesus' announcement of God's favour for unexpected people, and, so, they rejected him. His rejection in his hometown points ahead to his more brutal rejection in Jerusalem, his crucifixion and death. In the Gospel of Luke, Jesus is put to death because his broad, inclusive vision and practice is experienced as disturbing and threatening by many, especially by those who believed they had a special claim to God's favour. In spite of the hostile intent of the people of Nazareth, Luke states that 'Jesus passed through the midst of them and went on his way' (4:30). Luke thereby suggests that God's purpose at work in the life and ministry of Jesus will not be thwarted by hostile human purposes.

Luke's version of what we know as the Sermon on the Mount echoes the opening statement of his missionary programme in the synagogue of Nazareth (6:20–45). At the beginning of the sermon Jesus declares blessed the poor, the hungry and those who weep. Jesus declares this group 'blessed', in virtue of the promise that is made to them, 'yours is the kingdom of God', 'you will be filled', 'you will laugh'. When is this promise to be fulfilled? Luke is clear that the promise began to be fulfilled in the ministry of Jesus and in the continuation of that ministry in the Church. Jesus had declared in Nazareth: 'Today, this scripture is fulfilled in your hearing' (4:21). That little word 'today' is very important in the Gospel of Luke. When Jesus heals a paralytic in chapter five, the crowds say, 'We have seen strange things today' (5:26). Jesus will go on to say to Zacchaeus, 'Today, salvation has come to this house' (19:9). 'Today' is both the time of Jesus' ministry and the time of the Church when the risen Lord continues his work through the Holy Spirit.

One of the messages of Luke's Gospel is that, if the promises of God to the poor and the disadvantaged are to be fulfilled 'today', those of high social status must take appropriate action now. On one occasion, Jesus says to his wealthy host, 'When you give a banquet, invite the poor, the crippled, the lame, the blind' (14:13). Jesus calls on him to treat as family and friends those he would normally keep at arms length. If the wealthy do not heed this call, those on the margins will have to wait until the next life for their situation to be reversed. Such was the case with Lazarus in the parable of the rich man and Lazarus, one of many parables unique to Luke (16:19–31). In the Beatitudes, Jesus promises the hungry, 'you will be filled' (6:21). In this parable, Lazarus 'longed to be filled' but he was not. The hunger of Lazarus was only satisfied at the banquet in the next life, where he had the place of honour next to Abraham. The parable clearly indicates that Lazarus should not have had to wait that long. The Gospel of Luke emphasises that God's work of reversal must begin now. Luke describes the early Church as faithful to Jesus' kingdom mission of making present God's hospitality to those on the margins: 'There was not a needy person among them, for as many as owned lands or houses sold them and brought the proceeds of what was sold' (Acts 4:34). It is in this context that we have to hear the four 'woes' that are unique to Luke; they are addressed to the rich, those who are full, those who are laughing now and are spoken well of by all (6:24–5). The rich man in the parable of the rich man and Lazarus is representative of this group. He is so self-satisfied and self-absorbed that no other human being seems to cross his horizon. Another representative of the group to whom the 'woes' are addressed is the character in another parable unique to Luke, the parable of the rich fool (12:13–22).

There is an important verse towards the end of chapter nine that marks the moment when Jesus draws his ministry in Galilee to a close and begins to head in the direction of Jerusalem (9:51). Luke gives greater prominence to Jesus' journey to Jerusalem than the other evangelists. This journey occupies ten chapters of his Gospel, extending from 9:51 until Jesus' arrival in the city in 19:28. Luke opens this journey narrative in solemn tones, 'When the days drew near for him to be taken up, he set his face to go to Jerusalem.' At the end of his journey, Jesus will be 'taken up' to his father. In Luke's Gospel Jesus dies with the words, 'Father, into your hands I commend my spirit.' His journey to Jerusalem is his journey to the father. It is a journey he must take. Luke captures something of the firm determination of Jesus to face into a journey that would lead to rejection and death, recalling the determination of Isaiah, 'I have set my face like flint, and I know I will not be put to shame' (Is 50:7). Jesus sets his face to go to Jerusalem, where he will confront the power of privilege that leaves the majority of the people on the margins.

At the beginning of his Galilean ministry, Jesus experienced the rejection of the people of Nazareth. At the beginning of his journey to Jerusalem, he experiences the rejection of the Samaritans. The journey to Jerusalem begins as it will end, with the rejection of God's prophet. The one who reveals the God of great hospitality is refused hospitality by a Samaritan village, 'because his face was set towards Jerusalem' (9:53). After his rejection by the Samaritans, Luke tells us that Jesus 'went on to another village' (9:58). Undeterred, he continues his journey of making present God's hospitable love, in accordance with God's purpose. In Luke's second volume, the risen Lord offers God's hospitality again to the Samaritans, through his messenger Philip; this time they welcome the Lord with joy (Acts 8:8). The Lord does not reject those who reject him but continues to seek them out.

On the journey to Jerusalem, Jesus speaks many memorable parables that feature journeys that people make. In 10:25 a lawyer asks

Jesus the key question, 'What must I do to inherit eternal life?' Jesus encourages him to find the answer to his question within his own Jewish tradition: 'What is written in the law? What do you read there?' In response to the lawyer's second question, 'Who is my neighbour?' Jesus speaks the parable of the Good Samaritan. As people were listening to this journey story, they probably thought it was developing as an anti-clerical story. The priest and the Levite saw the half-dead man in need of help and pass by. Surely a Jewish lay man will now do the decent thing. However, the story is much more subversive than that. It is a member of the despised Samaritans who not only saw, like the priest and the Levite, but also 'had compassion'. This same kind of seeing has already been attributed to Jesus by Luke, in the story of the widow's son at Nain, a scene that is unique to Luke's Gospel, 'When the Lord saw her, he had compassion for her' (7:13). The Samaritan, the outsider, embodies Jesus' mission of bringing God's hospitality to the broken. The compassion of the Samaritan showed itself in a series of seven actions, symbolic of perfect service. The question that Jesus asked the lawyer at the end of the parable was not the lawyer's question, 'Who is my neighbour?' but 'Which of these three was a neighbour?' Jesus suggests that it is more important to become a neighbour than to ask, 'Who is my neighbour?' True neighbours do not ask that question, because their love does not discriminate. The person in need, whether family or enemy, calls on us to reveal God's boundless hospitable love. 'What must I do to inherit eternal life?' The parable suggests that the way to eternal life is to share in Jesus' ministry of offering God's hospitality to the broken and vulnerable, without making distinctions.

After the parable that portrays a Samaritan giving expression to the hospitality of God, Luke tells the story of the hospitality shown to Jesus by two women (10:38–42). Both women, who are sisters, offer Jesus hospitality, but do so in different ways. Martha expresses her hospitality by 'much serving', whereas Mary expresses her hospitality by taking up the posture of a disciple, sitting at Jesus' feet and listening to his word. She breaks with the social expectations of the culture by failing to help her sister with the domestic chores and, instead, just sitting at the feet of Jesus and listening to him. Martha's question to Jesus comes across as an accusation, 'Lord, do you not care …?' Jesus defends Mary's choice and gently and affectionately addresses himself to Martha's excessive and unnecessary anxiety. The passage presents Mary as offering a deeper hospitality to Jesus by attending to what the guest really wants. Mary has recognised who this visitor is and has received him with the loving attention that is appropriate.

Mary's attentive listening complements the compassionate activity of the Samaritan in Jesus' parable. Jesus will state in the following chapter: 'Blessed are those who hear the word of God and observe it' (11:28). By placing these two passages together, Luke may be saying that different forms of service are appropriate at different times. Some situations call for the service of activity, exemplified by the Samaritan, other situations call for the service of attentive listening shown by Mary. This passage is just one example of the significant role of women in both the Gospel of Luke and the Acts of the Apostles. The first person to hear the good news of the birth of the Messiah is a woman; the first people to hear the good news of the Resurrection of Jesus are women.

Closely linked to the theme of God's hospitality in Luke is the theme of table fellowship. The religious leaders were very critical of Jesus' eating style. At the beginning of chapter fifteen, Luke comments that 'the Pharisees and the scribes were grumbling and saying, "This fellow welcomes sinners and eats with them"' (15:1). In response to that criticism, Luke presents Jesus as speaking the parables of the lost sheep, the lost coin and the lost sons. The third parable is one of the great journey parables in Luke's Gospel. The younger son's request that the father give him the property due to him is like saying to the father, 'I can't wait for you to die.' His father's very existence is an obstacle to the son's goals. Having gotten what he wanted, the young son sets out on a long journey, full of expectation to conquer the world. Yet, his expectations were cruelly dashed. His decline into misery is graphically portrayed. The memory of his father is the beginning of his journey back from the edge. The speech he rehearses includes a confession of wrongdoing. What was said earlier of the Samaritan is now said of the father: he 'saw him and had compassion'. Just as the Samaritan is a Jesus figure, so too is the father. Both exemplify the lavish hospitality that characterises the ministry of Jesus towards those on the edge. The experience of his father's hospitality transforms the younger son; the lost one is found.

The hearers might have expected the parable to end there, in keeping with the two earlier parables; however, the story is not over. When the older son learns what has happened, he expresses his anger towards the father by refusing to enter the house. The father leaves the banquet to plead with his older son. Whereas the younger son would have been happy to be taken back as a hired servant, the older son had always thought of himself as a servant; he claims to have 'worked like a slave'. He had never really known his father as a loving father, more as a harsh, begrudging taskmaster. He has misjudged his father, who now addresses his elder son not as 'my servant' but as 'my son' and declares, 'All that is mine is yours.' The older son does not have to earn the father's property; it is already his. The story ends without it being said whether or not the older brother went back with the father to join in the father's hospitality towards his brother. The parable concludes in an open-ended manner.

The invitation goes out to all to join in the spirit of the acceptable year of the Lord, to recognise the crazy logic of God's hospitable love present in Jesus. The sons differ, but they both turned away from the father and both end up on the outside in different ways. The father is equally devoted to both sons. Such is the God revealed by Jesus in his ministry. The three parables of chapter fifteen could be understood as a commentary on Jesus' statement that 'the Son of Man came to seek and to save the lost', which concludes the Zacchaeus story. This statement also captures the essence of Luke's portrait of Jesus.

ADVENT

First Sunday of Advent

A season to renew our hope

Jer 33:14-16; 1 Th 3:12-4:2; Lk 21:25-8, 34-6

Today we begin the short season of Advent. We light the first candle on our Advent wreath. As the days continue to grow darker, the growing light of our Advent wreath over the next three Sundays proclaims that as a faith community we are drawing nearer to the celebration of that great feast of God's light, the feast of Christmas. By the time we get to Christmas day, the days will have begun to get imperceptibly longer, and our celebration of Christ's birth will coincide with the re-emergence of light within nature. In that sense, the lighting of our first Advent candle is full of promise, as we look ahead in hope to the coming of God's light in Christ and in nature.

The word 'promise' occurs in the first sentence of the first reading of the first Sunday of Advent today. It is a word that sets the tone for the whole season of Advent. The experience of broken promises can make us slow to trust the promises that people make to us. We do not always keep our promises. Our intentions can be good but we do not always follow through on them; however, as the prophet Isaiah says, God's ways are not our ways. God's word is not like our human word; God does what God says; God is true to God's promises. Advent is a season when we allow God's promises to make us hopeful.

Hope is more than optimism. Our optimism can be rooted in a whole variety of human circumstances. Hope can only be rooted in God; it is the human response to God's word of promise. Very often hope comes into its own when optimism dies. In the Gospel reading today, Jesus describes a scene that leaves very little room for optimism. He speaks of nations in agony, of people dying of fear, of threatening powers that menace the world and of disturbing signs in nature. Such a scenario would not encourage optimism. Yet, in spite of this grim scene, Jesus calls on his followers to be hopeful, to stand with heads held high. The reason for such hope amid this trauma is the coming of the Son of Man with power and great glory. Jesus promises that when all seems to be falling apart, he will come with his liberating power. This promise is the source of our hope.

Jesus is saying that even when there are no grounds for optimism, there is always reason for hope because God is stronger than the forces that threaten to engulf us. This is the heart of the Gospel message. Light shines in the darkness and the darkness cannot overcome it. There are evil forces at work in our world, in our own lives, but God's force for good, expressed through God's son and the Holy Spirit, is greater. Saint Paul expressed this conviction very succinctly when he said, 'Where sin abounds, grace abounds all the more.' It is this conviction that keeps us hopeful even in the face of great darkness and distress.

Hope never makes us passive; it always moves us to action. Because we believe that God is at work in even the most unpromising of situations we are encouraged to get to work ourselves. We can tackle even the darkest of situations because we know that God's light is in there somewhere, even if it is not apparent. The virtue of hope is a great gift to the Church and to the world. Hopeful people can inspire others to tackle what they might otherwise shy away from.

Advent is a season when we are invited to renew and deepen our hope. In today's Gospel reading, Jesus suggests to us how we can keep hope alive. He calls on us to 'stay awake, praying at all times'. The wakefulness or attentiveness to God that we call prayer helps us to remain hopeful. In prayer we become attuned to God's presence; we grow in our awareness of God's coming into even the most unpromising of situations.

Advent is given to us as a prayerful season; it is a contemplative moment in the Church's year. The summons of Jesus in today's Gospel reading is very much the call of Advent: 'Stay awake, praying at all times.' We might say, 'Who can possibly pray at all times? Surely, we cannot stop everything we are doing to pray.' Yet, Jesus is not asking us to withdraw from our day-to-day living. Rather, he is inviting us to be prayerful in the midst of our living, to become prayerfully attentive to the Lord's presence around us and within us at all times. This could be called a contemplative approach to life. Such a contemplative attitude which is attuned to the Lord's presence, his constant coming to us, can be nurtured by times of more focused prayer, moments of silence when we step back from everything and allow ourselves to hear the Lord speak to us in a more focused way. It is this prayerful attentiveness to the Lord's presence that keeps us hopeful, even in those times when all reasons for optimism seem to have gone.

Second Sunday of Advent

The call to come home to the Lord

Bar 5:1-9; Phil 1:3-6, 8-11; Lk 3:1-6

We are only a little over two weeks away from Christmas now and soon many of those who live abroad will be setting out on a journey home. The journey home for Christmas has become a great tradition around Christmas. People make an effort to be at home and to welcome others home at this time of the year. 'Home for Christmas' is one of the catch cries of the season. For those who cannot come home, great efforts are made to bring as much of an experience of home as possible.

That image of journeying home is very strong in today's readings. The long quotation from the prophet Isaiah in today's Gospel reading calls on people to prepare a way for the Lord, because the Lord is coming across the wilderness at the head of his people to lead them home to Jerusalem, the city from which they had been exiled. Those in exile were being assured that the Lord was coming to take them home. That image of people going home is even more prominent in the first reading. It is announced to the city of Jerusalem that the people who left the city on foot as slaves are soon to be brought back like princes, led by the Lord. God will guide the people home by the light of his glory.

In going home to Jerusalem, the people were, in a sense, going home to God, because Jerusalem was the city of God, the place where God had chosen to dwell. The temple in Jerusalem was the visible manifestation of God's presence. For us as Christians, Jesus is the new temple, the place where God is present and visible in a unique way; he is Emmanuel, God-with-us. As we approach Christmas, we too hear the call to journey home, to journey towards God, towards God's son.

At Christmas we will be celebrating the good news that God has made his home among us, in and through his son, who remains with us until the end of time. God came home to us through the birth, life, death and Resurrection of his son. If at Christmas we celebrate God's coming home to us, during Advent we hear the call to come home to God. Advent invites us to set out on a journey home, in the deepest sense of that word 'home', to set out on a journey towards God, towards Emmanuel, God-with-us. We may have left home in that deeper sense; we may have distanced ourselves from the Lord. Perhaps we have experienced life as something of a wilderness. In that wilderness we may have felt that God was distant from us and we, in turn, may have grown distant from the Lord. This Sunday, a voice cries in the wilderness, the voice of the Lord, calling on us to come home, to journey towards him.

The Christian life is always a journey. We will never be fully at home in this life, because our true home is in heaven. We are always journeying towards home, always moving towards the Lord. Paul assures us in today's second reading that this journey towards the Lord is not primarily our work. According to Paul, it is more fundamentally the Lord's work. That is why Paul prays that the Lord who began a good work in the lives of the Philippians would bring that good work to completion. The Lord works to bring us home to himself; the Lord draws us to himself. In the Gospel of John, Jesus says of himself, 'When I am lifted up from the earth, I will draw all people to myself.' The Lord's drawing is always prior to our journeying and it is the Lord's drawing us that will keep us journeying even when we seem to have very little energy to keep going.

In drawing us closer to himself, the Lord is always drawing us closer to each other. The Lord does not draw us to himself as individuals but as members of a people. Our journey towards the Lord, while very personal to each of us, is travelled with others. That is why in today's second reading Paul identifies God's good work coming to completion in us with our love for each other increasing more and more. The

Advent call to come home to the Lord is at the same time a call to come home to each other, to love one another as Christ loves us. As we approach the feast of Christmas we could ask ourselves what that might mean concretely for us here and now. Are there people I have drifted from that I need to connect with again? Is there someone I need to journey towards in love? There may be very particular journeys that the Lord is asking us to make at this time.

Emmanuel, God-with-us, is the living expression of God's journey towards us. We prepare to celebrate the feast of Emmanuel by journeying towards each other in love. In so doing, we can help to make the wilderness bloom for others. We can become the Lord's voice in their wilderness, people who enable others to recognise that the Lord is indeed present, even in the desolate and difficult moments when all seems lost.

Third Sunday of Advent
What must I do?

Zeph 3:14-18; Phil 4:4-7; Lk 3:10-18

There are certain questions in life that remain important to us all through our lives. One of those questions begins today's Gospel reading, 'What must we do?' What is the right thing, the good thing, to do? It is a question we will often find ourselves asking. If we have in our hearts the desire to do what is right, what is best, then that question will always be important for us. 'What must we, as a church, as a society, do? What must I do in my own personal life?' For us as followers of Jesus, as people who have been baptised into Christ, the question 'What must I do?' becomes 'What does the Lord want me to do?' 'What is the Lord asking of me?' The answer to that question won't always be easy to find. We may need guidance. We may need to talk to someone who can help us to see what it is we must do, what it is the Lord is asking of us here and now.

The people in today's Gospel reading looked to John the Baptist for guidance. He gave them very clear guidance. He called on everyone to share from their surplus with those in greatest need. Then he had specific guidance for specific groups. He told tax collectors not to defraud people, not to take more from them than was due. He told soldiers not to use their authority to intimidate people or to extort money from them. There was general guidance that applied to all and then there was specific guidance that was relevant to particular groups. John was aware that the call to share, to give of oneself to others, would find expression in different ways for different people, depending on their circumstances in life. That is true for all of us. The Gospel call is addressed to all of us in a general way, the call to love others as the Lord has loved us, to be generous in dealing with others as the Lord has been generous to us, to forgive as we have been forgiven, to serve as we have been served by the Lord. Yet, that general call will take a different concrete shape for each one of us, depending on the situation in which we each find ourselves. We each have to work out what the call of the Gospel means for us in our own specific circumstances of life: what must I do that no one else can do, that no one else is called to do, because my circumstances in life are unique to me?

What is the Lord asking of me personally, here and now? The second reading is taken from Paul's letter to the Church in Philippi. He wrote that letter from prison. If you read the entire letter, it is clear that Paul was asking himself in prison, 'What must I do?' What, in these very particular circumstances of my life, is the Lord calling me to do? You could say that his options were very limited as long as he was in prison. The experience of prison does not create many choices for people. Yet, Paul was aware that he had options. He could have retreated into himself and become completely self-absorbed. He could have become increasingly resentful. He did none of those things. Instead, he reached out to one of his churches, the church that had recently sent him help while he was in prison, the church in the city of Philippi. He managed to write a letter to them and to find someone to take it to them. It is a letter that is devoid of all self-pity and self-absorption. Instead it is full of pastoral care for the members of the Church who were going through their own valley of darkness in the form of hostility from the surrounding society. At one point he addresses them as 'you whom I love and long for, my joy and crown'. Even though his own situation was bleak, Paul reached out with love to those for whom he felt some responsibility. He knew what he had to do and, furthermore, he was empowered to do it. Towards the end of the letter he says, 'I can do all things in him who gives me strength.'

Paul can serve as an inspiration to us all. The snippet of his letter to the Philippians given to us this Sunday suggests the importance of prayer in helping Paul to discern what he had to do and in empowering him to do it. He says, 'If there is anything you need, pray for it, asking God for it with prayer and thanksgiving.' We look to the Lord in prayer to help us to discern what it is we must do, what it is he wants us to do. We look to the Lord not as someone who is removed from us, but as someone who, in the words of that same reading, 'is very near'. In the words of the first reading from the prophet Zephaniah, 'The Lord your God is in your midst.' If we open ourselves up to the Lord in prayer, he will guide and direct us as to what we must do and he will also give us the strength to do it.

Fourth Sunday of Advent
Being a blessed and graced presence

Mic 5:1-4; Heb 10:5-10; Lk 1:39-44

We are only two days from Christmas day. We all have last minute preparations to do for the feast of Christmas. Some of us may still have a present or two to purchase. Different people approach the arrival of Christmas day with different feelings. The children, of course, are looking forward to the coming to Santa. Many adults too will be looking forward to this special time and to what it means. Others may be less enthusiastic about the prospect of Christmas. Some may have had an experience of loss of one kind or another in recent weeks or in the past twelve months, and they sense that Christmas will only accentuate their sense of loss. Money may not be plentiful and the potential expense of Christmas can be a worry for some. Those who are prone to feeling lonely can feel lonelier over the Christmas time. It can be a difficult time for people living alone who may not get many visitors.

For that reason, paying visits can be such an important part of the Christmas time, especially visiting those who are living alone and who value a visit at this time of year. We will all be doing some visiting over the next few days. We will travel to meet up with members of our family or else they will travel to us. Some of us will head off on some journey or other on Christmas Day or St Stephen's Day or both to spend time with others. Visiting is one of the good traditions of Christmas. There is something about Christmas that makes us ask ourselves, 'Who do I need to visit at this time?' 'Who would benefit from a visit from me?' Indeed, in the run up to Christmas, not just over the Christmas period, a lot of worthwhile visits can happen. Some who have a musical gift might visit a nursing home and share that gift with people who might not normally experience live music. People have been benefiting from visits of one kind or another in recent weeks, and it will continue over the Christmas and probably into the new year. It is one of the good traditions of Christmas, the visit.

From that point of view, today's Gospel reading is very appropriate for this time of the year. It is the familiar story of Mary visiting Elizabeth. One young woman with child takes the initiative to visit her older relative who is also expecting a child. Luke's description of this meeting suggests that both women were greatly blessed by their coming together. Each woman was a source of blessing for the other. When Mary greeted Elizabeth, the child in Elizabeth's womb leapt for joy and Elizabeth herself was filled with the Holy Spirit. She and her child were blessed by Mary's greeting, Mary's presence. Not only was Mary a source of blessing for Elizabeth, but Elizabeth was a source of blessing for Mary. Elizabeth declared Mary blessed because of the child she was carrying and because she believed the promise made to her by the Lord. Luke describes a meeting which was truly grace-filled. Each of the two women brought the Lord's blessing to the other. They were each the better for having met the other. You could say that it is an example of human encounter at its best. Two people are present to each other in ways that reveal the Lord and allow the Lord to be present with all his gifts and blessings.

Perhaps that Gospel scene can help to remind us that it is our presence to each other that is important at this time of the year, rather than any presents we might purchase. Living Christmas well is about being present to others in ways that leave them blessed and graced. We all know from our experience that we are not always present to people in life-giving ways. We might be at a low ebb ourselves for some reason and we can have a disheartening and discouraging effect on others. Our encounters, even with those who mean most to us, don't always have the quality of the encounter between Mary and Elizabeth. Yet, it is good to be reminded of the difference we can make to each other by the way that we are present to one another. Each one of us can be a carrier of the Lord to others as Mary was a carrier of the Lord to Elizabeth. The Lord can work powerfully through each of us to bless and grace others. We tend to associate the giving of blessings with priests. Yet, because of our Baptism, we are all called to be a source of blessing for others, to be channels of the Lord's blessing to one another. We do that by the quality of our presence, by our attentive, loving, accepting, affirming, caring presence. Sometimes that will involve just naming the good in the other person. That really was what Elizabeth did for Mary. Elizabeth recognised Mary's trusting faith in the Lord and she named it, 'Blessed is she who believed.' Naming the good in the other is one of the ways that we can be a source of grace and blessing for them.

CHRISTMAS

Christmas: Midnight Mass
God's gracious love for all humanity

Is 9:1-7; Ti 2:11-14; Lk 2:1-14

One of the verses in Patrick Kavanagh's well-known poem, 'A Christmas Childhood', goes as follows:

> A water-hen screeched in the bog,
> Mass-going feet
> Crunched the wafer-ice on the pot-holes,
> Somebody wistfully twisted the bellows wheel.

It is a poem born of loneliness and solitude. Kavanagh penned it after spending a lonely Christmas in his flat in Dublin. He nostalgically looks back at the Christmases of his childhood in his native Monaghan. Christmas can be a lonely time for many people, those living alone, those who have been recently bereaved, those living far from home. Kavanagh's loneliness that Christmas turned out to be a truly generative and creative moment for him.

I was struck by the line, 'Mass-going feet crunched the wafer-ice on the pot-holes.' I find it very evocative. There may be less 'Mass-going feet' these days than there was when Patrick Kavanagh penned 'A Christmas Childhood'; yet, there is something about the feast of Christmas that brings people to Mass, especially on Christmas night. Christmas is a time when we feel the need to gather in various ways. Within our families we gather in each other's homes, around each other's tables. We gather with friends. Some of you will have been involved in organising different kinds of gatherings in the past few weeks, such as the gathering of the senior members of the parish community for a Christmas party. Many also feel the desire to gather in church at this time alongside others who are trying to follow in the way of the One whose birth we celebrate tonight.

Tonight's Gospel reading begins with a reference to a decree of the first Roman Emperor, Caesar Augustus, for a census throughout his empire, and it concludes with a heavenly host of angels praising God and announcing to some shepherds that God's favour was resting on all men and women. The birth of Jesus was overshadowed both by the presence of the Roman Emperor and the presence of heavenly angels. It was rooted in history and, yet, somehow beyond it. It happened at a particular time and place in human history, and, yet, it transcended that historical time and place. This child was born to a particular young couple, Mary and Joseph, in a small town on the margins of the Roman Empire, and yet he was also born to everyone in every generation and place. As St Paul puts it in tonight's second reading, 'God's grace has been revealed, and it has made salvation possible for the whole human race.' The birth of this child reveals God's gracious love for all humanity. The birth of a child to a young couple in the town of Bethlehem that night would impact the whole human race for every succeeding generation, down to our own time. The birth of Jesus has, in some way, touched all of our lives, which is why we have gathered together here in this church on this Christmas night, why we are happy to belong among those Mass-going feet.

Because of the birth of this child to Mary and Joseph in Bethlehem, we have all been greatly graced. God has given us the most precious gift he could give us, the gift of Jesus, the son of Mary and Joseph, but also God's own son. In coming among us through his son, God has, in a sense, become one of us. God has taken the shape of a human life, and in doing so God has shown what a human life at its best looks like, what it is to be fully human. Jesus reveals ourselves to us. He also reveals God to us. The son of Mary and Joseph allows us to put a human face on God. There was a strong conviction in the Jewish

Scriptures that people could not see God and live. Because God was so transcendent, so other, to see God was to die. Yet, through Jesus, God has become visible to us. When we look upon the face of God in Jesus, what we see is a face of love. That is why the message of the angel to the shepherds was, 'Do not be afraid. Listen I bring you news of great joy.' Joy, not fear, is to characterise our relationship with God. In the words of the heavenly choir of angels at the end of the Gospel reading, the birth of Jesus reveals God's favour towards us, 'Peace to all who enjoy God's favour.'

Perhaps one of the reasons we are happy to be among the Mass-going feet at Christmas time is that we sense that God has greatly favoured us through the birth of Jesus and his subsequent life, death and Resurrection, and we want to respond in some way. God has graciously favoured us, without asking us to earn that favour. 'God's grace has been revealed', in the words of Paul in the second reading. We are here tonight to give thanks to God for this favour. It is a night to allow ourselves to receive afresh God's favour, to open our hearts anew to the light of God's loving presence in Jesus, so that it penetrates whatever darkness we may find ourselves in. Christmas is the feast of God's closeness. It is a feast that can bring us closer to God. Tonight, we are invited to allow that to happen for us.

Christmas: Mass During the Day
Light in our darkness

Is 52:7-10; Heb 1:1-6; Jn 1:1-18

I am always struck by how easily children enter into the Christmas story and how well they announce it to us all. Perhaps that is because at the centre of the Christmas story is a family – a mother, a father and their child – not unlike the children's own families. Many of the children will have baby brothers and sisters, and they can relate easily to the baby who is the very heart of the Christmas story.

The word 'God' can suggest someone remote, very far above us, somewhat inaccessible; however, there is nothing more accessible than a newborn baby. Everyone wants to get close to a newborn baby. They inspire a certain fascination in all of us. We look at this new bundle of life, mesmerised. The parents who are here know that better than I do. Christmas celebrates the extraordinary good news that the newborn child of Mary and Joseph is God, God-with-us, Emmanuel. Those who looked into the eyes of this child were looking into the eyes of God. It is hard to imagine how God could have become more accessible to us than by taking the form of a newborn child. If God wanted to draw close to us, to engage us, to draw us into relationship, this was a very good way to do it. In Jesus, the firstborn child of Mary and Joseph, God became vulnerable, accessible, engaging.

Perhaps that is why the feast of Christmas continues to engage us at the spiritual level of our being. Yes, Christmas has become overly commercialised. We all spend more than we need to; if we are not careful we can easily go overboard. Yet, the numbers who come to church on Christmas Day are always higher than other times of the year. God who reached out to us through a newborn baby continues to draw us at this time of the year. It somehow feels right to come to church on this day of all days. It is as if we sense, at some level, that if

God has gone to such lengths to connect with us, the least we can do is attempt to connect with God. Like the shepherds, we hear the call to come to the crib. On reaching it, we are invited to let our eyes and our minds roam free as we ponder the wonderful mystery of Jesus' birth, the mystery of Emmanuel, God-with-us.

Mary and Joseph's child, of course, became an adult, a vigorous young man who placed his life's energy at the disposal of God the Father for the service of all men and woman. As the adult Jesus went on to say, 'The Son of Man came not to be served but to serve and to give his life as a ransom for many.' He gave his life for us all, and, having been raised from the dead, he continues to give himself to us all. Indeed, at this Eucharist, which we now celebrate, the risen Lord gives himself to each of us as the bread of life. We come here on this Christmas morning not only to ponder the image of the child Jesus in the crib, but to receive into our lives in the Eucharist the glorious and risen adult Jesus. He calls us who are adults into an adult relationship with him. He says to us what he said to his disciples on the night before he died, 'I no longer call you servants ... I call you friends.' He waits for us to reciprocate, to befriend him as he has befriended us, to reach out towards him as he has reached out towards us, to accept him as our companion on our life's way.

The second reading this morning from the letter to the Hebrews speaks of God's son as 'the radiant light of God's glory'. When John the evangelist wanted to express the mystery of this feast of Christmas, he wrote, as we heard in today's Gospel reading, 'A light ... shines in the darkness, a light that darkness could not overpower.' The adult Jesus in the Gospel of John speaks of himself as the light of the world and promises that those who follow him will never walk in darkness. Many of us today experience a sense of darkness in one form of another. It might be the darkness of depression, of illness, of a broken relationship, of a deep loss, or the darkness that envelopes us when we look at all that is not right with our world and, perhaps, with ourselves. At Christmas we celebrate the coming of Jesus as light into our darkness. On this Christmas morning, we might make our own that wonderful prayer of John Henry Newman, a great scholar and writer of the nineteenth century, an Anglican who became a cardinal of the Roman Catholic Church. It is a prayer that has been put to music and is addressed to the risen Jesus as light in our darkness:

Lead, kindly light, amid the encircling gloom,
lead thou me on;
the night is dark, and I am far from home;
lead thou me on.
Keep thou my feet; I do not ask to see
the distant scene; one step enough for me.

The Holy Family of Jesus, Mary and Joseph
Pondering the mystery

1 Sm 1:20-2, 24-8; 1 Jn 3:1-2, 21-4; Lk 2:41-52

The Sunday after Christmas is a very good time to be celebrating the feast of the Holy Family. Christmas is very much a family time. Most of us try to make some effort to connect with our family members at Christmas time. There is something about Christmas that brings us together as family. That is also true of the wider family of believers we call the Church. There is something about the feast of Christmas that brings together the members of the family of faith. Moving beyond the Church family to the human family, Christmas is a time when we become more aware of the members of the wider human family, especially those who are in greatest need. There is no doubt that Christmas draws great generosity from people. Charities are the beneficiaries of such generosity at this time of the year.

We have such a stronger sense of family at Christmas time – of our personal family, of the Christian family and of the human family – because at the heart of the feast of Christmas is a family. Jesus was born into a family, a family that consisted not just of Mary and Joseph but of many other relatives as well – grandparents, aunts, uncles and cousins. Today's Gospel reading makes reference to Jesus' 'relations and acquaintances'. Referring to Jesus' family as the 'holy family' can make them seem rather remote from us. Yet, Jesus' family was a human family, like any other family of the time in many ways. The Gospels suggest that the people of Nazareth, Jesus' hometown, did not see his family as all that different from their own. When Jesus went back to Nazareth as an adult to preach his Gospel, the people of his town asked, 'Where did this man get all this? … Is not this the carpenter, the son of Mary and the brother of James and Joses and Judas and Simon, and are not his sisters here with us?' They were really saying, 'He is just like us, so how come he seems to have all this wisdom and is capable of performing all these mighty deeds?' As a baby, as a child, as a teenager, as a young adult in Nazareth, Jesus did not stand out as all that different to others of his age. In a small town like Nazareth at that time, everyone struggled to survive, and Jesus and his family would have been no different. His father, Joseph, had a skill that he passed on to his son and that they both used to try and make ends meet.

The story about Jesus' family we have just heard in the Gospel reading describes an experience that is not all that far removed from the experience of families today. Jesus was twelve years of age. In the Jewish culture of the time that was the age when children began to take on the responsibilities of adulthood. The Gospel reading suggests that Jesus began to show an independence of spirit at the age of twelve. As devout Jews, his parents had brought him to Jerusalem for the great feast of Passover. They returned from Jerusalem with their extended family, relatives and acquaintances, presuming that Jesus was somewhere among this wider family network. Not a bit of it! He had stayed behind in the temple. He was fascinated by the teachers of God's law that he found there. The Gospel reading says he was listening to them and asking them questions. His questions emerged from his listening. If Jesus was fascinated by these learned men, they were astounded at his intelligence and his replies. Jesus, it seems, was lost in a world that his parents did not inhabit to the same degree. When his parents finally found him, the exchange between Jesus and his parents highlights the extent to which they were on different wavelengths. Addressing Jesus, Mary refers to 'your father and I', meaning Joseph and herself. In reply, Jesus refers to 'my Father', meaning God. Even at this young age it seems that Jesus knew himself to be subject to a higher authority than his parents.

The Gospel reading says that his parents did not understand what he meant, but, nonetheless, Mary stored up what Jesus had said in her heart. She didn't dismiss what he said but mulled it over in her mind and heart. Perhaps there are lessons here for us all today in our dealings with each other, whether it is blood family members or those who belong to the wider families of the Church or of humanity. We don't easily understand one another; we remain strangers to one another. There was clearly a mysterious quality to Jesus, which his parents would have been most aware of, but there is a mysterious quality to each one of us. Just as God was clearly at work in Jesus' life from an early age, God is at work in all of our lives. Sometimes all we can do is respect the mystery of each other, and, like Mary, learn to ponder that mystery which we will never fully grasp.

Solemnity of Mary, Mother of God
The Lord present in our experience

Num 6:22-7; Gal 4:4-7; Lk 2:16-21

I always find that there is something about the turning of the year, New Year's Eve, New Year's Day, that makes me reflective. I find myself looking back over the year that has gone and looking ahead to the year that is coming. Perhaps we all engage in that kind of reflection at this time. Some people looking back on the year just past will think to themselves that it was a very difficult year; they are glad to see it go and they are hoping that the year to come will be easier. Others looking back over the past twelve months might find themselves with a sense of gratitude for all the blessings that came their way during the year. For some of us, the past year may stand out because of some celebratory event; for others, it is an experience of loss and sadness that dominates the year. As people of faith, we try to see the past, whatever form it has taken, from a particular perspective. We try to recognise the presence of the Lord in all that has happened to us. It can be easier to recognise his presence in the celebratory experiences than in the painful and distressing ones; yet, he has been there in all of our experience.

Part of the journey of faith is learning to recognise the presence of the Lord in all of our life experience, without exception. At the heart of the message of Christmas is that God has become flesh. All of human experience is charged with the presence of God. To recognise the Lord's presence in all that happens to us, we need a certain kind of attentiveness to our lived experience. Today, we celebrate the feast of Mary, the Mother of God. She is portrayed in today's Gospel reading as having that quality of attentiveness to her experience. When the shepherds arrived from the fields to the town of Bethlehem and found Mary and Joseph and their baby lying in a manger, they repeated to everyone present the wonderful message that the angels had delivered to them. The Gospel reading says that everyone was astonished at what the shepherds had to say; however, only Mary 'treasured all these things and pondered them in her heart'. She kept turning over within herself what the shepherds had said. In this way, she came to recognise the presence of God in these strange and unexpected events that were happening in her life. She is portrayed in the Gospel reading, and elsewhere in the Gospels, as a contemplative woman who silently holds in her heart mysteries she could not fully understand at the time. She was quietly unwrapping God's gift of her child with all its implications.

We have all learnt a great deal from our mothers. Often it is our mothers who teach us the most important lessons in life. Mary, the mother of Jesus, the mother of God, is also the mother of the Church, the mother of believers, and, perhaps, what we can learn from her at the beginning of this new year is the importance of acquiring a contemplative approach to all of our experience. Like her, we are called to ponder on all that happens to us so as to begin to recognise the presence of the Lord there. I am very fond of that blessing in our first reading today from the book of Numbers, 'May the Lord bless you and keep you. May the Lord let his face shine on you and be gracious to you.' It is one of several wonderful Jewish blessings in the Jewish Scriptures. I often find myself praying this blessing for someone. As Christians, we believe that the Lord has let his face shine on us and has been gracious to us in an extraordinary way in and through the birth of Jesus, who is Emmanuel, God-with-us. This same Jesus, as risen Lord, promised to be with us always, until the end of time. His face is constantly shining upon us; he is always being gracious to us. The contemplative attitude, exemplified by Mary, allows us to recognise the face of the Lord shining upon us, even in the darkest of our experiences; it enables us to become aware of the many ways the Lord is being gracious to us, even at those times when it seems as if he might have abandoned us.

We walk in the light of the Lord's presence, at all times. Saint Paul would go further and say that we carry that light deep within us. In today's second reading, Paul tells us that God has sent the Spirit of his son into our hearts, crying, 'Abba, Father!' The Spirit of God resides deep within us and, as Paul reminds us in that reading, through that Spirit we are caught up in Jesus' own relationship with God, becoming sons and daughters of God. As such, we can call God 'Abba, Father', as Jesus did. This is our baptismal identity. It remains true for each one of us, regardless of where we are on our life journey. There is a great deal to contemplate here. Like Mary, we too have many things to treasure and much to ponder in our hearts this coming year.

Second Sunday after Christmas
Word becoming flesh

Sir 24:1-2, 8-12; Eph 1:3-6, 15-18; Jn 1:1-18

The Vatican Observatory is an astronomical research and educational institution located in Vatican City and supported by the Holy See. Why the Vatican would support an observatory is a question commonly asked. In a recent interview, the director of the Vatican Observatory said the reason the Vatican supports an observatory is very much linked to the feast of Christmas. At Christmas, we celebrate the extraordinary news that God chose to become part of the created universe. Today's Gospel reading puts it very simply and very profoundly: 'The Word became flesh; he lived among us.' The Word who is God became human flesh – without ceasing to be God – in the person of Mary and Joseph's child. The director of the Vatican Observatory explains that in becoming part of the created universe, in becoming flesh, God shows us that this physical universe matters greatly. It matters so much that God chose to be part of it. The careful study of this universe, of God's creation, which is what we call science, thereby becomes an act of worship. The director goes on to say that 'astronomy is not only an appropriate activity for a church to support, it is also right for individual humans to spend their whole lives doing it, if given the chance'. The baby in the manger, he says, gives importance and meaning to all the physical activity of the universe.

The Word, in becoming flesh, teaches us to value the physical universe and the work of scientists who devote themselves to studying that universe. In becoming flesh, the Word did not simply become part of the physical universe. More specifically, the Word who is God became human, taking on a human nature. If our human nature was good enough for God to embrace, then we should highly value our human nature. We also value the efforts of all those who work to try and understand our human nature more fully, those who devote time and energy to understanding how our body works, how our mind functions, the role our emotions play in our lives, and the spiritual dimension of our human nature. The Incarnation, the Word becoming flesh, gives an added significance to all those human sciences that seek to understand who we are. Just as the study of the planets and the physical universe can be an opening onto God, so the study of the human person in all his or her dimensions can be an opening onto God, because Jesus has shown that human nature has the capacity to be a powerful revelation of God. The Word became flesh.

In becoming flesh, God is inviting us to become alert to the ways that the physical universe and, in particular, human nature, the human person, can be powerful revelations of God. Because God is Creator, it is when we as humans are at our most creative that we reveal God most fully. All those involved in the creative arts have a wonderful opportunity to reveal God to us and to help bring us into an experience of God. Looking upon a painting can be a very spiritual experience. If the artist is in some way open to the divine spirit, his or her work can draw us into an experience of the divine. Some of the paintings of the artist Caravaggio come to mind. I can never look upon his depiction of the call of Matthew without feeling myself called in some way. Some creative artists work in stone or in other materials. Their work too can have a spiritual quality that allows us to be touched by God. Musicians are another example of creative artists who make it possible for us to sense the divine. The Swiss theologian, Karl Barth, once said: 'When the angels sing for God, they sing Bach; but I am sure that when they sing for themselves, they sing Mozart – and God eavesdrops.' Many great artists of all kinds have been aware of themselves as channels for God's energies. What is true of musicians and artists is equally true of poets and novelists, those who give expression to their creativity in word. Some of the poems that I learned in secondary school have stayed with me into adult life, and I believe it is because those poems had a spiritual quality to them. The poet was somehow open to divine inspiration.

Because of the Incarnation, the Word becoming flesh, God can work powerfully in and through all of our lives. Our own flesh can be, and often is, a revelation of God. Saint John in his first letter wrote, 'God is Love.' When he writes that the Word, who is God, became flesh, he is really saying that God's love became flesh. As we go about our daily lives, whenever we give of ourselves in love to someone, God's love continues to become flesh in us. Whenever we give without expecting a return, whenever we share our resources, our gifts, our time, our energy, so that others can live a fuller life, God's love is becoming flesh in us.

The Epiphany of the Lord
Seeking after truth

Is 60:1-6; Eph 3:2-3, 5-6; Mt 2:1-12

The Gospel story that lies behind today's feast has captured the imagination of people throughout history. Artists and storytellers have been inspired by it, as have poets. There is even an operetta inspired by this story, called *Amahl and the Night Visitors*. The story of the three wise men speaks to the imagination of children. Perhaps one of the reasons why this story speaks so powerfully to us and appeals so strongly to us is that we recognise something of ourselves in this story.

How would Matthew, the evangelist, have understood these strangers from the East? The Gospel story does not refer to them as 'kings'. That was a later interpretation. The Gospel story also doesn't say that there were three. This was a deduction from the fact that three gifts were offered to the child Jesus. The evangelist refers to them as 'magi', men who had some expertise in the area of astrology or astronomy. Such people were often associated with Persia, far to the East of Israel. Their fascination with the stars could strike a cord with people of all faiths and no faith. I have never seen a sky at night from a desert where the air is totally clear and where there is no artificial light. That would have been a normal experience in the time and place of Jesus. The stars inspire an endless fascination in people. Many explored the world of the stars for some understanding of what was happening on earth. It was commonly believed, for example, that the birth or death of some significant leader was marked by an unusual phenomenon in the heavens, such as the appearance of a comet. For the evangelist, these magi were seekers. They were exploring the heavens to better understand the world of human beings. They were seekers after truth. We might struggle to identify with kings. Very few people get to be kings. Yet, we would find it easy to identify with seekers after truth, understanding, wisdom. We are all seekers in that sense. We want to know the truth about ourselves, about others, about our world, about God. We are always on a journey towards the truth. We never fully grasp it in this life; it is always to some extent beyond us.

The Magi's search for the truth eventually brought them to the child of Bethlehem, to the one who, as an adult, said of himself, 'I am the truth,' and who declared, 'If you continue in my word ... you will know the truth, and the truth will make you free.' The ultimate goal of our search for the truth is also the child of Mary and Joseph who is now our risen Lord. Our whole life is a journey towards that fullness of truth, revealed in Jesus. He reveals to us the truth about ourselves as human beings, the truth about this earthly life and the heavenly life beyond it, and the truth about God. When the Magi reached the end of their long journey, when they saw the child and his mother, their initial response was to worship the child, 'Falling to their knees, they did him homage.' Our journey's end, which lies beyond this earthly life, will also be one great act of worship. Every act of worship during our journey towards that final destination is a foretaste of that eternal worship in heaven. The second action of the wise men when they reached their journey's end was to give him the gifts that were most precious to them. Our own journey's end in eternity will also be an act of self-giving. Our worship will be so pure that it will entail the giving of ourselves completely to the Lord. We will have the freedom to give back to God everything God has given us. In the course of our earthly journey, every time we generously give back to God what God has given to us, through our service of others, we are anticipating that eternal moment of self-giving.

There is much about the journey of these Magi from the East with which we can identify, not least their struggle to reach their goal. Their journey from the East to Bethlehem was not a straight path. It had twists and turns. Along the way they encountered someone who wanted to destroy the very truth for which they had been so earnestly seeking. When King Herod heard of the arrival in Jerusalem of these strangers from the East, looking for the infant king of the Jews, alarm bells rang. He was the only king of the Jews. He summoned the wise men and played games with them. He pretended he wanted to worship the child, when, in reality, he wanted to kill him. Here was untruth personified. Yet, Herod could not stop God's epiphany. On our own journey towards the Lord, we too will encounter forces that are hostile to our search for Jesus, the truth. Our faith will be put to the test. Yet, we can be confident that if we keep our eyes fixed on the Lord, he will bring us to our destination. In the words of Paul's letter to the Romans, nothing 'in all creation will be able to separate us from the love of God in Christ Jesus our Lord' – and that includes the various Herods of this world.

The Baptism of the Lord
Jesus in solidarity with us

Is 40:1-5, 9-11; Ti 2:11-14, 3:4-7; Lk 3:15-16, 21-2

The Baptism of Jesus by John the Baptist is represented at least twice in our parish church. It is to be found in mosaic form in the reconciliation chapel and in the reredos behind the altar. In a church dedicated to John the Baptist, it is not surprising to see that Gospel scene more than once. There was something unusual about Jesus coming to John the Baptist for Baptism. After all, John's Baptism was a Baptism of repentance for the forgiveness of sins, and those who came to him for Baptism did so confessing their sins and looking for God's forgiveness. Surely, Jesus had nothing to confess and was in no need of God's forgiveness; yet, he joined that throng of sinful humanity who made their way to John by the Jordan river. Jesus was standing in solidarity with all those who knew themselves to be sinners and were looking for God's forgiveness. This would set the tone for Jesus' ministry to follow. Having been baptised alongside sinners, he would go on to share table with them and would end up being crucified between two criminals.

In coming to John for Baptism, Jesus was showing that he wanted to journey with us in all our brokenness and frailty, in all our proneness to failure and sin. We may be inclined to think that the Lord only has time for us if we first get our life in order. Nothing could be further from the truth. Jesus did not ask people to change for the better before he engaged with them. In engaging with them as they were and revealing what today's second reading calls 'the kindness and love of God' to them, he empowered them to change. Jesus spoke of himself as the doctor who sought out the sick; he said he had come not to call the righteous but sinners. There are times in our lives when we might think that we have given the Lord good reason to distance himself from us. It is above all at those times that he is in solidarity with us, walking with us, just as he walked with all those who set out to submit to the Baptism of John. We can find it hard to believe that this is how the Lord relates to us, perhaps because we tend to relate to one another rather differently. We often distance ourselves from those who have offended or hurt us. We pull back from those in whom we have invested but who have failed to live up to our expectations. This is often the human way, but as the prophet Isaiah says, the Lord's ways are not our ways. The conclusion of today's first reading captures the way of the Lord very graphically. He is like a 'shepherd feeding his flock, gathering lambs in his arms, holding them against his breast'.

God showed his approval for this way of Jesus, for his walking in solidarity with all those who journeyed to John in the Jordan. At Jesus' Baptism, God's Spirit, the Holy Spirit, descended upon him, and he heard God say to him, 'You are my son, the beloved, my favour rests on you'. Jesus was bathed in God's favour at his Baptism, and he was bathed in God's favour so that he could be a channel of that favour to all people. Jesus would spend the whole of his public ministry bringing God's favour to all who were open to receiving it. He remains the channel of God's favour to all of us here today. Our own Baptism was a privileged moment when we were the recipients of God's favour through Jesus. Today's second reading declares that the kindness and love of God was revealed to us through the cleansing water of rebirth, through the generous pouring out of the Holy Spirit upon us. In and through our Baptism, God said to us, 'You are my son, my daughter, the beloved; my favour rests on you.' On the day of our Baptism, most of us would not have had any real awareness of such divine favour because we were infants. It is only as we get older that we can begin to appreciate the meaning of our Baptism. It can take each of us a very long time to really hear and believe those words of God as spoken to us personally, 'You are my beloved; my favour rests on you.' It is above all during those times in our lives when we are aware of ourselves as having failed and fallen short that we most need to hear those words as addressed to us.

Our Baptism sets the tone for all of our lives. What God said to us on the day of our Baptism, he says to us every day of our lives. That is why we say, 'I am baptised', rather than, 'I was baptised'. Baptism gives us our identity as God's beloved sons and daughters on whom God's favour rests. That is why we are only baptised once, and then we spend our lives embracing our Baptism and all it means. Jesus' Baptism was the beginning of his mission of revealing the kindness and love of God to all. That is our baptismal calling too. Like Jesus, we are called to share with others the favour of God which rests upon us.

LENT

First Sunday of Lent

Faithfulness to God's calling

Deut 26:4-10; Rm 10:8-13; Lk 4:1-13

We all get a certain satisfaction from discovering shortcuts. In this fast-moving world we often ask, 'What is the fastest way from A to B? What is the quickest way to get this done?' We have gotten used to doing some things much more quickly than we would ever have done them in the past. In no area of life is this truer than in communications. Communications that once took days or even weeks now take seconds. We benefit greatly from this increased efficiency; however, we also know that when it comes to the more important things in life, there are no shortcuts. Time and patience, faithfulness and application are required and cannot be substituted.

In today's Gospel reading Jesus is tempted to take a variety of shortcuts. His mission was to lead people to God. Satan suggests a number of shortcuts that Jesus could take to ensure that his mission gets quick results. He could use his power to turn stones into bread and thereby become a kind of one-man bread basket for the people of Palestine. He would have people eating out of his hand – literally – and then he could lead them anywhere he wanted. Alternatively, if Jesus were to worship Satan, he would be given authority and power over all the kingdoms of the world. From such a position of power, he could influence and control people in any way he wished. Or else, knowing that God would protect him, he could perform a series of heroic feats without getting hurt, like throwing himself down from the pinnacle of the temple. Such circus-like acts would be great entertainment and would have people flocking to him in large numbers.

Jesus resisted those temptations because he knew that there was no shortcut for what God had sent him to do. There was no easy way of doing God's work. Indeed, Jesus was well aware that his mission of revealing God's love and justice to Jews and pagans, of gathering people together into a new family under God, would necessitate the way of the cross, the way of suffering, rejection, humiliation and death. There was no other way, if he was to be faithful to the mission that God had given him.

The temptations that we find in today's Gospel reading were somewhat unique to Jesus as the Christ, the son of God. Yet, they are not without relevance to all of us. Like Jesus, we too have been baptised, and like him we too received a calling and a mission on the day of our Baptism. We are called to follow Jesus and to reveal him to others. That involves setting out on a journey that does not lend itself to shortcuts or to easy options. Following Jesus today will often mean taking the road less travelled, saying 'no' to what seems very attractive and beguiling. When Jesus was saying 'no' to the shortcuts that Satan was suggesting to him, he was really saying 'no' to putting himself first. Rather than putting himself first, he emptied himself, taking the form of a servant. That is our calling too. As we begin Lent, we are asked to look at ways we might become less self-serving and more the servant of others. In today's second reading Paul reminds us that our baptismal calling is to confess Jesus as Lord, not just on our lips but in our hearts, with our lives. To confess Jesus as Lord is to live as his servants, to empty ourselves for others as he did. This will often mean going the long way around for the sake of others rather than taking the shortcut, going the extra mile with someone who needs our companionship and support.

In today's Gospel reading, Jesus was saying 'no' to the temptation to compromise himself for the sake of getting quick results. He would, instead, set out on a path that would not bring quick results. On the contrary, as he hung dying from the cross, it appeared that his mission would have very little, if any, results. Yet, he had sown a small seed and it would go on to become a large shrub. His life would ultimately bear rich fruit. Jesus, thereby, teaches us that faithfulness to God's calling is a more important value than instant success, as this world measures success. If we allow Jesus to be Lord of our lives, then our lives too will bear rich fruit, both for ourselves and for others, even if they don't appear to be successful in the way that success is often measured today. In our struggle with temptation, we have the same resource to help us that Jesus had. According to the Gospel reading, Jesus entered the wilderness 'filled with the Holy Spirit'. That same Spirit has been poured into our hearts at our Baptism. In the wilderness, Jesus drew inspiration from the word of God every time he was put to the test by Satan. That same word of God has been given to us, a word which, according to Paul in the second reading, 'is very near to you'. In our own testing times, we can pray in the words of today's psalmist, 'My refuge, my stronghold, my God in whom I trust!'

Second Sunday of Lent
Seeing more deeply

Gn 15:5-12, 17-18; Phil 3:17-4:1; Lk 9:28-36

Towards the end of my time in secondary school I noticed I could not see the writing on the blackboard very well. I went to an optician and discovered that I needed glasses. As I have gotten older, the prescription for the glasses has gotten gradually stronger. Some years ago, I ended up with bifocals. Needing ever-stronger glasses is part of the aging process for some of us.

There are different forms of seeing. There is physical sight and then there is a deeper kind of seeing, where we see below the surface of things. Some kind of light comes on in us and we see in a new way. We often refer to these experiences not as moments of sight but as moments of insight. Perhaps this is the kind of seeing with which the disciples were gifted in today's Gospel reading. They had been with Jesus for some time. They had seen him heal the sick, share table with all sorts of people, feed a multitude in the wilderness; however, on the mountain, they saw Jesus in a way they had never seen him before. The Gospel reading says that they saw Jesus' glory. They saw beneath the surface of his life to the person he truly was. They saw him in all his full reality. He was more than a wonderful human being; he was the son of God. The disciples on the mountain were graced with an ability to see the personal reality of Jesus unveiled. Peter wanted to prolong it, 'Let us make three tents ...' However, this was an experience that could not be bottled. It could not be frozen. It was a momentary gift; it could be savoured for the moment. Yet, the memory of this experience could sustain the disciples for the difficult road ahead as they walked behind Jesus, who was soon to set his face to go to Jerusalem.

There are times in our own lives when we can be graced in a way that is similar to how Peter, James and John were graced on the mountain. We may think we know someone well. Then we get a sudden and momentary insight into some dimension of their being. It is as if we see them more deeply than we have ever seen them before. We sense that these moments of insight come to us as a gift. We are not aware of having done anything to make them happen. They are given to us and, yet, every gift has to be received and, so, in some sense, we have been receptive to this gift. The gift of seeing Jesus in a way the disciples had never seen him before came to them in the context of prayer. Jesus had taken Peter, James and John up the mountain to join him in prayer. In our own lives, a prayerful spirit can dispose us to receive this momentary grace of seeing people in all their full reality, indeed, in their glorious reality, as people made in the image and likeness of God. Seeing someone in this deeper way once is an experience that can live on in our memory, to be called upon when we might be tempted to see them in a much more surface way.

This deeper seeing can impact not only on how we see other people but on how we see all of reality. When we look at a certain situation in life in a purely surface way, we might see it as a problem and no more than that; however, when we open ourselves to the grace of seeing the situation more deeply, we can come to discover that the problem is also an opportunity that calls out to us. There is a sacramental quality to all of life. The Word became flesh and dwelt among us. The flesh of life, all of it, reveals something of the Word who is God. God is revealed in all of our experience. The Word of God speaks to us through all of our human experience, even those dark experiences that seem devoid of God's light. There is a spiritual quality to all of life and the Lord will give us eyes to see this deeper dimension to all things if we are open to this gift.

The Gospel reading invites us to reflect not only on how we see others and how we see life, but how we see ourselves. In that second reading, Paul tells us that our ultimate destiny in eternity is to be transfigured, so that we finally become copies of Christ's own glorious body. There is a sense in which this transfiguration is already underway through the work of the Holy Spirit in our lives. As Paul says in one of his other letters, 'We are being transformed into the same image [the image of the Lord] from one degree of glory to another.' Something of the same depth that the disciples saw in Jesus on the mountain is to be found in each one of us if we have eyes to see.

Third Sunday of Lent
There is hope for a tree

Ex 3:1–8, 13–15; 1 Cor 10:1–6, 10–12; Lk 13:1–9

There has been just a little sense of spring in the air recently. The days are getting noticeably longer. Those who have gardens may have started to think about going out into them and doing some preparatory work in advance of the summer. Soon people may start heading out into the garden to uproot one or two shrubs that have not survived the winter and to replace them with new shrubs straight out of one of the garden centres.

The owner of the vineyard in the parable that Jesus speaks in today's Gospel reading had the same idea. He instructs his gardener to dig up a fig tree, and with good reason. This particular tree had not given figs for three years. Here was a tree that was taking in nutrients from the soil for three years and over that time had given nothing back. Most would conclude that its fruit-bearing days were over and that it was just taking up space; however, in the story Jesus tells, the gardener convinces the owner of the vineyard to give the tree one more year, during which time every effort will be made to get it to bear fruit. The gardener was clearly a patient man; he believed that all was not lost, even when all seemed lost.

In Jesus' parable, it is often the case that one of the characters is an expression of himself and of God. In the parable of the Good Samaritan, the figure of the Samaritan is an image of Jesus and of the God Jesus reveals. In our parable today, the gardener is an image of Jesus and of God. Throughout the Gospel Jesus shows himself to be patient with those that others would write off or even cut off. Once when a blind beggar called out to Jesus and his disciples told him to be quiet, to make himself invisible, Jesus cut across his disciples and called the man over. On another occasion, when Jesus was refused hospitality by a Samaritan village and his disciples wanted to call fire down from heaven and consume them, Jesus rebuked his disciples and went on to another village. Jesus knew that a time would come when the Samaritans would hear his Gospel and receive him. He knew how to wait for people; he had patience when it was needed.

The risen Lord knows how to wait for all of us. There are times when our lives do not appear to be very fruitful. The many and varied graces that the Lord may have given us over the years appear to yield very little return. We can probably all think of times in our lives when we were not at our best, when we were a little bit like the fig tree in today's parable. There may even have been times when we were tempted to give up on ourselves, knowing that we were a long way from the person we are called to be. Today's Gospel reading assures us that the Lord is slow to give up on us, even when others may be tempted to do so. The Lord continues to invest in us, even if past investments have given little return. The Lord is patient. It is, of course, true that the Lord's patience should not make us complacent. As Paul says in today's second reading, 'The one who thinks he is safe must be careful that he does not fall.' Rather, the Lord's patience makes us hopeful. The gardener in today's parable had hope for an apparently hopeless tree. The Lord has hope for us; he is always hopeful in our regard, which is reason enough for each of us to be hopeful in our own regard. We also need to be hopeful in each other's regard, knowing that the Lord who began his good work in us is always working to bring it to completion.

If the Lord continues to invest in us, we need to invest in ourselves. There is always something we can do in response to what the Lord is doing. We have a more proactive role in our future than the tree in the parable had in its future. There may be a little pruning we can do on our own lives, a little nurturing, that enables the Lord's work in our lives to be more effective. That is the other side of today's Gospel reading, the call to repent, the call to turn away from whatever it is that is diminishing us and to turn towards what is truly life-giving for us. Moses in the first reading might be our inspiration in this regard. In the wilderness, while he was going about his business as a shepherd, he heard the Lord's call and he replied, 'Here I am.' In the midst of his daily task, he suddenly found himself on holy ground. The Lord calls out to all of us as he called out to Moses and whenever we try to respond to that call we too begin to walk on holy ground. Lent is a good time to listen more attentively to the Lord's call and thereby to create an opening for him to make our lives rich with the Spirit's fruit.

Fourth Sunday of Lent

Coming in from the cold

Jos 5:9-12; 2 Cor 5:17-21; Lk 15:1-3, 11-32

When we go to a film or a play that has a range of different characters, we can sometimes find ourselves identifying with one of the characters. Something about a particular character speaks to us; it might be the situation in which they find themselves, or their reaction to that situation. Identifying with one of the characters allows us to enter into the story more fully. The parable that Jesus tells in today's Gospel reading is one of the best known of Jesus' parables. It is a story that has spoken to believers down through the centuries. It has inspired some of the greatest artists. We only have to think of Rembrandt's *The Return of the Prodigal Son*, which depicts the reunion of the father and his younger son who arrives home a broken man from the distant country towards which he had earlier set out with such great expectation. It is this particular moment in the story that has captured the imagination of artists like Rembrandt. In many ways, that moment of encounter between the loving father and his rebellious son is the high point of the story.

Yet, on hearing this story, many people find themselves drawn to the third character, the elder son. We somehow identify with him. It is through the elder son that many of us find ourselves entering the story. We often feel a certain sympathy for this dutiful, hard-working son who resents all the fuss that is being made over his younger brother who had walked away from his duties and responsibilities to indulge his own desires without any regard for others in the family. We sense that justice is not being done here because the self-indulgent son is getting what he does not deserve and this person of exemplary character seems to be getting a raw deal. Many of those who first heard the parable from Jesus' own lips may well have responded to it in just this way. It is that last part of the story, the meeting between the elder brother and his father, that often engages us more powerfully, which is why the traditional title of this story, *The Parable of the Prodigal Son*, does not really do it justice. It is not just a story about one son, but a story about a father and his two sons.

Anger is the emotion that characterises the older son: 'He was angry and refused to go in.' He refused to have anything to do with the homecoming celebrations that his father had ordered for his younger son. Perhaps the elder son had more anger towards his father than towards his younger brother. The anger of the older son towards his father in the story was a mirror image of the anger of the Pharisees and the scribes towards Jesus. 'This man', they said of Jesus, 'welcomes sinners and eats with them.' Like the elder brother in the story, they too were asking why those who had not kept the rules were now being showered with such grace and favour. To some extent, in speaking this parable, Jesus was really saying that his ways, God's ways, are not our ways. The attitude of the elder brother towards his younger brother corresponds more to our ways; that is why we find it so easy to identify with him. The attitude of the father towards his younger son corresponds more to God's ways. The story suggests that God's sense of justice and our sense of justice are not quite the same. There is a generosity of spirit about the father that explodes the rather strict sense of justice that characterises the elder brother, and, often, ourselves. The same generosity of spirit characterised Jesus, and the God revealed by Jesus. In reading and reflecting on this story, I find it helpful to ask myself the question, 'If I were the younger son returning home, who would I prefer to be there on the doorstep waiting to receive me, my father or my older brother?' Or to put the question in another way, 'If I were the younger son, whose sense of justice would I be more at home with, that of the father or that of the elder son?'

The parable could be heard as inviting us to move more in the direction of God's ways, to become more like the father and less like the elder brother. If anger characterised the elder son, compassion was the hallmark of the father. In the words of the Gospel reading, 'While he was still a long way off, his father saw him and was filled with compassion.' The parable calls on us to make the journey from anger to compassion whenever those who have done wrong take steps to put things right and to make a new beginning. The son who stood in judgement over his father and his younger brother was not as virtuous as he made himself out to be. Like his younger brother, he too needed to come home, to come in from the cold. We all have to make that same journey; none of us have arrived. We are all sinners. That realisation can help us to create a space for the generous spirit of the Lord to grow more fully within us.

Fifth Sunday of Lent
Honest to God

Is 43:16-21; Phil 3:8-14; Jn 8:1-11

It is often the case in life that what appears to be going on in some situation is not what is actually going on. Somebody may appear to be worked up about one thing, but in fact they are worked up about something else. The presenting issue is not always the real one. This is because often we find it easier to come at something in a roundabout way than to come at it directly.

We have a good example of this in today's Gospel reading. The scribes and Pharisees come to Jesus with a woman who had been caught in the act of committing adultery. On the surface it appeared that their focus was the woman. They wanted to know from Jesus how the Jewish law should be interpreted in her regard. Their real focus, however, was not the woman but Jesus. As the Gospel reading says, they asked Jesus their question as a test, looking for something to use against him. If Jesus were to say that the Jewish law should not be followed, they could accuse him of being a law breaker. If he were to say the Jewish law should be followed, he would lose his reputation as a friend of sinners. The real interest of the scribes and Pharisees was to set a trap for Jesus. The woman was simply being used as bait.

The evangelist presents Jesus as knowing what they were really up to. He recognised their hypocrisy. They appeared as conscientious upholders of the law; in reality, they were out to undermine Jesus so as to protect their own position. Jesus refused to answer their question because he saw that it was not a real question. His writing on the ground suggests an unwillingness to play their game. When they persist with their questioning, Jesus eventually cuts through their hypocrisy with his probing invitation, 'If there is one of you who has not sinned, let him be the first to throw a stone at her.' Their subsequent slipping away showed some awareness that they were not without sin themselves. Whereas the scribes and Pharisees used the woman, Jesus treated her with great respect. He declared first that God was not condemning her; he then called her to live in a way that was in keeping with her dignity as someone made in God's image.

The Gospels indicate that Jesus was very intolerant of hypocrisy. He valued openness and honesty, both in people's dealings with each other and in their dealings with God. On one occasion he said of Nathanael, 'Here is truly an Israelite in whom there is no guile.' Nathanael's earlier remark, 'Can anything good come out of Nazareth?' was an honest expression of his prejudice. We often say that with certain people 'what you see is what you get'. We mean that as a compliment; we recognise a certain openness and honesty in them. We appreciate such qualities in people because, even if we do not agree with them, at least we know where we stand.

Another Gospel character that appears to have that lack of guile is Peter. He does not pretend to be someone he is not; on one occasion he said to Jesus, 'Depart from me, I am a sinful man.' In response, the Lord called him to share in his mission, 'From now on it is people you will catch.' The Lord looks to us to be open and honest in our own dealings with him. He asks us to pray as we are, for example, rather than as we think we should be or as we imagine the Lord might want us to be. One opportunity to be open and honest with the Lord is in the Sacrament of Reconciliation. There we can reveal ourselves to the Lord as we are, confident that he has no difficulty dealing with honest sinners.

The Lord not only wants us to be open in our dealings with himself, but in our dealings with each other. A lack of openness with others and the readiness to use others often go hand in hand, as today's Gospel reading shows. Many people come to feel used because someone was less than open and honest with them. We are called to be as honest in our dealings with each other as the Lord has been with us. On one occasion in the Gospel of John, Jesus says: 'I have spoken openly to the world … I have said nothing in secret.' We know that we all have a long way to go in being as guileless with each other as the Lord has been and continues to be with us. We can easily identify with Paul's sentiments in today's second reading, 'Not that I have become perfect yet. I have not yet won, but I am still running.' We still have a journey to travel in our efforts to be more like Jesus and less like the scribes and Pharisees. We also know that our efforts are only part of the picture; the Lord is also at work in our lives. In the words of today's first reading, he is always doing some new deed within us and among us. Our calling is to allow his good work to come to completion in us.

Palm Sunday

Overcoming evil with good

Is 50:4-7; Phil 2:6-11; Lk 22:14-23:56

We have just heard the story of the last hours of Jesus of Nazareth as told by Luke. It is this story that we will be reflecting upon in the coming week, the only week in the Church's year that is called Holy Week. The story we have just heard is in one sense tragic, the story of the cruel execution of an innocent man. Luke's telling of the story goes out of its way to declare the innocence of Jesus. Pilate declares Jesus innocent no less than three times, 'I have found no case against him.' One of those crucified with Jesus declares, 'This man has done nothing wrong.' The centurion, seeing how Jesus died, proclaims, 'This was a great and good man.' Jesus dies as the innocent victim of a grave injustice. Therein lies the tragedy of the story we have just heard.

There have been many innocent victims of grave injustices since then. There may have been times in our own lives when we felt that we were unjustly treated. Such experiences can leave us feeling angry and resentful. One of the extraordinary features of the story we have just heard is that the injustice done to Jesus did not fundamentally change him. He retained his goodness, his love for others, right to the end. He remained the person he had been all his life, even as he unjustly endured so much hostility and hatred. Luke details Jesus: healing the ear of one of those who came to arrest him; turning to look compassionately at Peter at the moment Peter denied him for the third time; praying aloud asking God to forgive those who were executing him; and, in the final words he spoke to another human being, promising paradise to one of the criminals crucified alongside him. Here was the triumph in the midst of the tragedy, the triumph of goodness over evil, of love and mercy over sin and injustice. I am reminded of St Paul's words in his letter to the Church in Rome. 'Do not be overcome by evil, but overcome evil with good.'

Luke's story of the last journey of Jesus reminds us that our greatest triumph lies in how we relate to others, regardless of how they relate to us. We have little control over how others treat or regard us. We have some control over how we respond to the way others relate to us. If, with the help of the Holy Spirit, we respond in the way Jesus did, then we share in his triumph. When we retain our goodness, our integrity, in the face of forces that threaten to diminish us and violate our dignity, then the Lord's triumph, the triumph of this Holy Week, takes flesh in our own lives. The story of Jesus becomes our story, and the love of God which Jesus revealed most fully in the hour of his passion and death is revealed in our lives.

Sacred
Triduum

Holy Thursday
Receiving the Lord's love

Ex 12:1–8, 11–14; 1 Cor 11:23–6; Jn 13:1–15

All four Gospels agree that Jesus was crucified on a Friday, the day before the Jewish Sabbath. All of the Gospels agree that, on the previous evening, Thursday evening, Jesus had a final meal with his disciples. We call that meal the Last Supper. We commemorate the Last Supper every time we celebrate Mass; however, at this Holy Thursday evening Mass, we commemorate the Last Supper in a very focused way. That is why only this Holy Thursday Mass is called the Evening Mass of the Lord's Supper.

The earliest reference to the Last Supper, the oldest reference, is to be found in this evening's second reading. In that reading, Paul reminds the Church in Corinth of the tradition about that Last Supper that he had earlier passed on to them by word of mouth, when he first preached the Gospel among them, 'This is what I received from the Lord, and in turn passed on to you'. The remembrance of that Last Supper was one of the most precious traditions of the Church. It was a precious tradition because of what happened at that Last Supper, what Jesus did. However, in that reading, before describing what Jesus did at the Last Supper, Paul refers to what was done to Jesus. Paul initially refers to that evening as 'the night he [Jesus] was betrayed'. This was the dark side of that evening. One of Jesus' closest disciples, one of the Twelve, one of that group in whom Jesus had invested so much of himself, betrayed Jesus that evening. Yet, the shadow that was cast over that evening did not define it. It was not defined in the memory of the early Church by Judas' act of betrayal. It was instead defined by Jesus' act of love. It is that act of love that we commemorate and celebrate this Holy Thursday evening.

What was that act of love? There were indeed two acts of love that defined that evening. One is described by the evangelist John in this evening's Gospel reading and the other is described by the apostle Paul in this evening's second reading. The first of Jesus' acts of love we will re-enact in a few moments. Very often, in the culture of Jesus, a host would give his guests a bowl of water to wash the dust of the streets and paths off their feet. It was considered a fitting act of hospitality. It would never happen that the host himself would wash the feet of his guests. If the host was wealthy, he might get one of his slaves to wash their feet, but he would never do it himself. What Jesus did at that Last Supper in washing the feet of his guests, his disciples, was something completely out of the ordinary. It was totally unconventional. Peter's reaction to what Jesus was doing was perfectly understandable, 'You shall never wash my feet.' Yet, Jesus' insistence was stronger than Peter's resistance. This was how Jesus wanted to relate to his disciples. He wanted to serve them in this very menial way, as it would have been understood then. He wanted to empty himself in their service. He was treating them with great respect and dignity. He was giving himself in love for all of them, Judas included. We have to see those disciples as representing all future disciples, all of us here this evening. The way Jesus relates to them is how he wants to relate to us all. The Lord's self-emptying love embraces us all. In laying aside his garment to empty himself in love for his disciples, Jesus was anticipating what he would do on the following afternoon. Then, his garments would be taken from him by his enemies and Jesus would empty himself in love on the cross for all of humanity.

This evening we celebrate the extent to which Jesus gave of himself for us all, at the Last Supper and on the cross. We are invited to do what Peter was so reluctant to do, to receive the Lord's love in the way the Lord wanted to express it. Having received that love, we are then invited to share that love with each other. In washing the feet of his disciples, Jesus was showing us how we are to relate to one another. We are to approach each other with the same respect for the dignity of the other that Jesus showed on that evening.

The second action of Jesus on the evening of the Last Supper is described by St Paul in the second reading and by the other three evangelists, Matthew, Mark and Luke. He took bread, thanked God for it, broke it and gave it to his disciples, saying, 'This is my body, which is for you.' He took a cup of wine, thanked God for it, and gave it to his disciples, saying, 'This cup is the new covenant in my blood.' Jesus identified himself, his body and blood, with the bread and wine. Just as he gave himself in love to his disciples by washing their feet, he now gave himself in love to them under the form of bread and wine. Just as in washing their feet, he anticipated the gift of himself he would make on the cross, so in giving them his body and blood under the form of bread and wine he was again symbolically anticipating the gift he would make of himself on the cross.

The members of the early Church repeated this second action of Jesus, with his accompanying words, every time they gathered to celebrate the Eucharist. At every Eucharist, the love to which Jesus gave expression by his actions at the Last Supper and most fully on the cross is present again to us all. As Paul says at the end of that second reading, 'Every time you eat this bread and drink this cup, you are proclaiming the Lord's death', and the love which the death expressed. At every Eucharist, we are invited to receive the Lord's love and we are called by the Lord to bring the love we have received to each other. At every Eucharist, the Lord sends us out with the words, 'Love one another, as I have loved you.'

Good Friday
Jesus' greater love

Is 52:13–53:12; Heb 4:14–16, 5:7–9; Jn 18:1–19:42

Good Friday is the only day in the Church's year when Mass is not celebrated. In a few moments we will receive communion that was consecrated at yesterday evening's Mass. Mass is a joyful act of thanksgiving, but today there is a restraint about the Church's worship because we are remembering Jesus' death. We gather at this time on Good Friday to remember the Lord's death because, according to the Gospel, Jesus died at the ninth hour, our 3 p.m.

Yet, even though our liturgy this afternoon is sombre, we don't gather in sadness. After all, it is Good Friday. Yes, bad things happened to Jesus on that Friday. Judas handed Jesus over to the religious leaders, who then handed him over to Pilate, who in turn handed him over to his soldiers to be crucified. Jesus was deserted by most of his disciples, betrayed by one of them, and publicly denied by the leading disciple. He was the innocent victim of the worst instincts of people. There was a great deal that wasn't right about what happened on that Friday. Sin and evil left a terrible mark on Jesus. Yet, we still refer to that day as Good Friday, because we don't remember so much those worst instincts of human nature that were to the fore on that day. We remember, rather, the way Jesus responded to what was done to him. We remember his love, which shone all the brighter against that dark backdrop.

We have just read the passion narrative according to St John. Earlier in the Gospel of John, Jesus had said, 'No one has greater love than this, to lay down one's life for one's friends.' It is that greater love of Jesus that we are remembering and celebrating this afternoon. Jesus' greater love was, in reality, a revelation of God's love for all of humanity. Again, in the words of the John's Gospel, 'God so loved the world that he gave his only son.' Jesus had spent his public ministry serving others. His death was the final and full expression of that life of service. He lived for others and, now, he died for all of us, for each one of us. Each of us here this afternoon can say with St Paul in his letter to the Galatians, 'I live by faith in the son of God who loved me and gave himself for me.' It is 'love' that we are remembering and celebrating this Good Friday afternoon, God's love revealed in the death of Jesus and in the lives of his followers.

Wherever we find the kind of self-emptying love that Jesus embodied, it is always life-giving for others. The Church has always believed that there was something uniquely life-giving about the death of Jesus, about the love of Jesus that his death expressed. In the passion narrative we have just heard, after Jesus died a soldier pierced Jesus' side with a lance, and immediately there came out blood and water. Both blood and water were symbols of life in the Jewish world. The blood and water that flowed from the side of Jesus is an image of the life-giving power of his death. Jesus' death was life-giving for all of us. Earlier in the Gospel of John, Jesus speaks of himself as the good shepherd who lays down his life for his sheep, so that we may have life and have it abundantly. Jesus gave up his earthly life out of love for us to draw us into communion with himself and with God. Insofar as we allow Jesus to draw us into communion with himself and with God, we will become fully alive as human beings in this earthly life, and we will inherit eternal life beyond this earthly life. When we gather at 3 p.m. on Good Friday it is not to recall the human hatred that brought death, but rather the divine love that brings life.

We are invited this afternoon to stand with those characters in the story who were receptive to the love that shone through Jesus and the life it offered. Who were those characters? You will find them at the foot of the cross, that little community of Mary the mother of Jesus, Mary the wife of Clopas, Mary Magdalene and the disciple

Jesus loved, that nameless disciple who represents us all. This little community of faithful love recognised in the darkness of that day a light that darkness could not overcome, a love that was stronger than hatred and sin, a death that offered new life to all. This group of five were, in a sense, the beginning of the Church, to which we all belong. We are invited to see the death of Jesus with their eyes, eyes which recognise the cross on which Jesus hung not just as an instrument of torture but, in the words of today's second reading, as 'the throne of grace'. It is because we see the cross in this way that we will soon come forward to venerate it.

Easter Vigil
A hopeful feast, a hopeful people

Rm 6:3-11; Lk 24:1-12

There was something quite dramatic about the beginning of our liturgy this evening. We enter a dark church with just the light of the Easter candle. Gradually the light from the Easter candle spreads throughout the Church and in the light of our candles the Easter hymn of praise is sung. That dramatic entrance rite before the Liturgy of the Word is fitting on a night when we celebrate a drama of momentous proportions. Tonight, we are celebrating God's drama in raising his son from the dead on that first Easter morning. We are here tonight because we feel that we have all been caught up into that drama. What God did on that first Easter morning has touched all of our lives. We recognise that the light of that first Easter Sunday has continued to shine down through the centuries and is shining upon us tonight. It is the light of a life that is stronger than death, of a love that is stronger than hatred and sin. Because of what happened on that first Easter morning we can say, with St Paul, 'Where sin abounds, grace abounds all the more.'

That is why Easter is such a hopeful feast and why we decorate our churches with beautiful flowers after the barrenness of Lent. It is because of Easter that we are a hopeful people. There are many reasons for despair in our world today. The problems of the world, even of our own lives, can seem beyond any solution and can easily leave us disheartened. Yet the great lesson of the first Easter Sunday is that God can bring new life out of death, God can turn the awful tragedy of the killing of his own son to the good of all humanity. In raising his son from the dead, God released a power for good into the world, a power of life. We call this power the Holy Spirit. It is this spirit which allows us to say with St Paul, 'I can do all things through him who strengthens me.' That is the dynamism of this feast of Easter which we are invited to imbibe.

Yet, the Gospel reading this evening suggests that those who were around on that first Easter morning did not pick up on this hopeful spirit immediately. I am struck by the three different reactions to the events of the first Easter Sunday that are presented in our Gospel reading. It is said of those faithful women that when they went to the tomb on that first Easter morning, they stood there 'not knowing what to think'. It seems to me a very human reaction, one that, perhaps, resonates with all of us. We can get our head around the feast of Christmas easily enough; we have all had some experience of the birth of a child. But, what are we to make of Easter? Like the women we stand there 'not knowing what to think'. What happened on that Easter morning never happened before. It was outside the realm of ordinary human experience. It was as if God's world invaded our world in a way that left everyone confused, 'not knowing what to think'. This was God's extraordinary surprise. Death has finally been defeated, not just for Jesus but for all of us who open ourselves in faith to this risen Lord. Who could have seen that coming?

There was a second response to those events mentioned in the Gospel reading. When the women told the eleven and those who were with them what they had seen and heard at the tomb of Jesus, the Gospel reading says that the story 'seemed pure nonsense' to the eleven male disciples and they did not believe the women. There are many today who would consider the Easter story to be pure nonsense, a figment of people's imagination, some kind of wish fulfilment. This is what Jesus' disciples wanted to happen, so they made it happen. Yet, this is such an inadequate response to the extraordinary event of that Easter morning. It is saying that because we cannot fully understand an event it must be nonsense.

There is a third response mentioned in the Gospel reading. Peter responded to the women's story in a different way to the other ten disciples. He ran to the tomb of Jesus to see for himself. We are told that having seen, 'he went back home, amazed at what had happened'. Amazement is not yet Easter faith but it is on the way to it. Indeed, it remains an essential part of Easter faith. Easter should never cease to amaze us. Nathanael once said, 'Can anything good come out of Nazareth?' Many of Jesus' disciples must have asked despairingly, 'Can anything good come out of Golgotha?' To that question God gave a resounding 'yes' on Easter Sunday morning and that 'yes' will always amaze us. Easter is such an amazing feast that the Church gives us seven weeks to reflect on it, up until Pentecost Sunday. During Lent many of you may have done the Stations of the Cross. During this season of Easter, we travel what has come to be called the Stations of Light, those Gospel texts which tell the story of the many appearances of the risen Lord to his disciples. This is the hopeful journey we are being invited to take during these coming seven weeks.

EASTER

Easter Sunday Morning
The insight of love

Acts 10:34, 37–43; Col 3:1–4; Jn 20:1–9

Many of us would say that the people who know us best are those who love us most. Those who have given themselves in love to each other over many years and who have remained faithful to each other know each other in a way that no one else knows them. Those we claim to know we often do not really know because we have no real connection with them. We don't love them enough to really know them.

In the Gospel of John one of Jesus' disciples is always referred to as the disciple that Jesus loved. The fourth evangelist believed that there was a very special bond between Jesus and this disciple. Here was a disciple who was completely open to the presence of God's love in the person of Jesus and who responded fully to that love. For the fourth evangelist, this disciple is the ideal disciple, the disciple we are all called to become. He is portrayed in the fourth Gospel as someone who, because of his special bond of love, knew Jesus better than any of the other disciples. Here was someone whose knowledge of Jesus was born of a greater love. He saw more clearly and more deeply than others. In today's Gospel reading, he alone saw the true significance of the empty tomb of Jesus. In the words of the Gospel reading, 'He saw and believed.' On the basis of the empty tomb alone, he recognised that Jesus had been raised from the dead. The other disciples came to this realisation only after the risen Lord had appeared to them.

What the beloved disciple recognised, what he believed, is what brings us together here on this Easter Sunday. God has raised his son to new life. This is the heart of our Christian faith. As St Paul says in his first letter to the Corinthians, 'If Christ has not been raised, then our proclamation has been in vain and your faith has been in vain.' This statement was made by someone who a few verses earlier in that same letter had declared, 'Last of all, as to one untimely born, Christ appeared also to me.'

If Jesus had not been raised from the dead, his life and work would have been a glorious, but nonetheless tragic, failure. Without Jesus' Resurrection from the dead, what he began would have petered out. The Resurrection was God's resounding 'yes' to all that Jesus said and did, to all that he lived and died for. Because of Jesus' Resurrection, we can recognise his life and his death as the manifestation of God's love for all humanity and the revelation of God's will for our lives. The Resurrection has been described as the keystone without which the entire archway of our Christian faith would collapse. That is why Easter, and not Christmas, is the most important feast in the Church's year. That is why the season of Easter is seven weeks long, running right up to the feast of Pentecost, whereas the feast of Christmas is only twelve days long.

We celebrate this great feast of Easter with flowers and song and alleluias not only because it has to do with Jesus, but because it has to do with all of us. Christ's triumph over death is also our triumph. We all share in Christ's triumph over death through our Baptism. On the day of our Baptism, we were plunged into Christ's risen life. As Paul says in his letter to the Romans, 'The Spirit of him who raised Jesus from the dead dwells in you.' The Holy Spirit, the spirit of the risen Lord, received at Baptism, is the first fruit of that fullness of life that Jesus now lives and that we are all destined to inherit. Because Jesus has been raised from the dead, all of us who have been baptised and are united with him through faith are Easter people. We live in the light of Easter, no matter how deep the darkness that may envelope us at times.

If you were to find an image of the Christian life in today's Gospel reading, it would not be the sad journey of Mary Magdalene to the tomb in the darkness; it would be much more the excited running to the tomb of the beloved disciple and Peter in the early light or, even more so, the subsequent journey of Mary Magdalene who, having met the risen Lord, went to the disciples to announce, 'I have seen the Lord.' Because of Easter, because of our conviction that in the person of Christ life has triumphed over death, we can approach with expectant faith whatever it might be in our life that seems to be a tomb, trusting that signs of new life are to be found there. Because of Easter we know that even our darkest moments, our Golgotha experiences, are bathed in the light of the risen Christ. Because of Easter we are also sent forth, like Mary Magdalene, as messengers of the risen Lord. Easter commits us to resisting all forms of death and violence; it commissions us to be channels of God's vibrant life to all who are in darkness and the shadow of death. In renewing our Baptism on this Easter day, we renew our response to that Easter commission.

Second Sunday of Easter
Not seeing, yet believing

Acts 5:12–16; Rv 1:9–13, 17–19; Jn 20:19–31

In Robert Browning's poem, 'A Death in the Desert', the last of the apostles, John, is dying. He looks back over his life and he wonders what will happen after the death of the last person to know Jesus personally. He asks what will happen when:

> 'there is left on earth
> No one alive who knew (consider this!)
> —Saw with his eyes and handled with his hands
> That which was from the first, the Word of Life.
> How will it be when none more saith "I saw"?'

The question being asked in the poem is, 'What will happen when there is no one left who can say "I saw the Lord"? When all the eye witnesses of the Lord die off, what then?'

How can people who have never seen him believe in the Lord? That was the dilemma that faced Thomas in today's Gospel reading. His fellow disciples came to him full of joy, having seen the risen Lord for themselves. They had been locked in a room out of fear, but suddenly they were aware of the risen Lord standing among them, giving them the gift of his peace, and empowering them to share in his work through the Holy Spirit. They came from this transforming encounter with the risen Lord to Thomas, one of their number, who was not present when the Lord appeared. Thomas was being asked to believe without having seen, to believe on the basis of what his fellow disciples were telling him. He refused to do so. If they had seen, he wanted to see as well. He not only wanted to see the risen Lord, but he insisted on physically touching the wounds on Jesus' hands and side.

Unless these conditions were fulfilled, Thomas declared, 'I refuse to believe.' He wasn't going to be swept up by the enthusiasm of the other disciples. He wanted physical proof that Jesus was alive.

There is something admirable about Thomas' dogged scepticism. There is a tremendous honesty about it. He drove a hard bargain with the other disciples and with the Lord. Thomas' attitude left him somewhat isolated. He was cutting himself off from the group of disciples. It might seem as if he was also cutting himself off from the Lord. Yet, it is clear from the Gospel reading that the Lord was not cutting himself off from Thomas. A week later the risen Lord appeared to the disciples again, this time with Thomas present. Jesus' opening words to Thomas were not words of rebuke but of invitation, 'Doubt no longer but believe.' The Lord was accommodating himself to Thomas' sceptical stance. We are being reminded that the Lord meets us where we are and calls out to us where we are. The fact that someone's scepticism places them somewhat outside the community of believers does not mean that it places them outside the Lord's concern. In his scepticism, Thomas remained a seeker. He undoubtedly wanted to share the Easter faith of his fellow disciples but he could not bring himself to do so. Yet, the Lord considers everyone who is a seeker and who sincerely wishes to believe as a believer already. All the Lord needs is some level of openness, no matter how small.

What is probably the greatest confession of faith in Jesus in all of the four Gospels now comes out of the mouth of the great sceptic. When Thomas saw the Lord, he exclaimed, 'My Lord and my God.' He recognises Jesus in his full reality, as Lord and God, and does so in a very personal way, '*My* Lord and *my* God.' The deepest faith is often found in those who have lived through a period of great spiritual darkness, a time of doubt and unbelief. There is an element of doubt in all our believing; we all journey through life enveloped in darkness to some degree. Even the great St Paul could say, 'Now, we see in a mirror, dimly.' Some seem to have a much stronger encounter with that spiritual darkness than others. In a way, Thomas is their patron saint. He shows that times of disturbing and isolating religious doubt can be the prelude to deeply rooted and richly expressed faith.

Eventually Thomas saw and believed, like the other disciples who saw the risen Lord and believed. However, what about us who have not seen the Lord in the way that those original eyewitnesses saw him? That brings us back to the question of Robert Browning's poem, 'How will it be when none more say "I saw"?' Yet, here we are, a gathering of those who believe without having seen. It is to us that Jesus addresses the final beatitude in all of the Gospels, 'Blessed are those who have not seen and yet believe.' Jesus acknowledges that our faith is every bit as genuine as the faith of the original eyewitnesses, those who saw and believed. Even though we haven't seen, our faith is not without foundation. It rests on the faith of those who saw and believed, which is preserved for us in the Gospels and the other writings of the New Testament. Even more fundamentally, it rests on the presence of the risen Lord to us in and through his Church.

Third Sunday of Easter

Jesus on the shore of our failure

Acts 5:27-32, 40-41; Rv 5:11-14; Jn 21:1-19

Most of us have had to cope with failure in one form or another in the course of our lives. As a young person, we may have failed some examination; later in life, a relationship that was important to us may have broken down or a project that we put a lot of ourselves into may have come to nothing. We will also have known moments of personal failure, when we failed to live up to our own values. The experience of failure can sometimes be quite devastating. We may find it hard to pick ourselves up from it. Yet, we have to find ways of moving on from it. We cannot allow it to define us. It is never the whole story of our lives.

The story we have just heard in today's Gospel reading is set within the context of failure. The group of disciples who went fishing in the dark of night caught nothing. These were experienced fishermen who knew the Sea of Galilee well, and yet their labours that night proved to be fruitless. That experience of professional failure had followed on from a moment of great personal failure for all of them. Having left their nets and their boats to follow Jesus, having spent time in his company, they deserted him just as he began to enter into his final journey, his passion and death. Simon Peter had denied Jesus very publicly three times. Only the disciple whom Jesus loved had stayed by the cross with the women. After this traumatic experience of personal failure, the only option open to them was to go back to their fishing. Yet, they seemed to have lost the ability to do even that well.

This story of failure begins to take a turn for the better with the statement of the evangelist, 'It was light by now and there stood Jesus on the shore.' Jesus, whom they had deserted, was standing by them. His first words to them were not accusing words; rather, he spoke to them as fishermen, initially asking a question and then making a suggestion that resulted in a huge catch of fish. This turn for the better in their fortunes as fishermen was a prelude to a turn for the better in their fortunes as disciples. The risen Lord had come to renew their discipleship rather than their careers as fishermen. When the beloved disciple identified the stranger on the shore as the Lord, Simon Peter, in particular, lost interest in the great catch of fish, and jumped from the boat into the water towards the Lord. He must have sensed that his own recent failure as a disciple was not the end of the road after all.

Jesus went on to have breakfast with his disciples. With the simple gesture of sharing food, he showed that he wanted to remain in communion with them and was inviting them to renew their communion with him. Jesus' subsequent question to Simon Peter, 'Do you love me?' gave Peter the opportunity to renew his own personal communion with the Lord, after which the Lord conferred a new responsibility on Peter with the words, 'Feed my lambs … feed my sheep.'

Whenever we fail, we need people to stand by us. When we fail professionally, we need people who can help us to look at our situation with new eyes, who can point us in a new direction, prompting us to throw our nets to the other side of the boat, as it were. When we experience some more personal failure, we need people to stand by us all the more. At such times, we value people who can help us to see that there is much more to us than our failure. We appreciate greatly those who can name the good in us that we can easily become blind to at such times. When we struggle to believe in ourselves, we often need other people to believe in us, if we are to keep going. The simple invitation from someone to share table, 'Come and have breakfast', can mean a great deal to us when our world appears to be collapsing. Such moments of communion have a sacred quality to them; they are one expression of what we might call holy communion.

Those who are present to us in this way reveal the Lord to us. Today's Gospel reading assures us that at times of failure the Lord stands on the shore of our lives. As risen Lord, he is constantly coming to renew the communion that we may have broken with him. He calls us to his table, even when we have denied or deserted him. As he does so, he asks us the question that matters most to him, 'Do you love me?' It is a question that invites us to put the Lord first in our lives, to make our relationship with him our primary relationship. The living out of that relationship will always involve feeding the Lord's flock, caring for others, especially in their moments of greatest vulnerability. His invitation to Peter, 'Feed my lambs ... feed my sheep' is addressed to us all. The Lord calls us to have a pastoral responsibility for each other. We are to reveal to each other something of the love of the good shepherd who laid down his life for us so that we might have life to the full.

Fourth Sunday of Easter
Listening and following

Acts 13:14, 43–52; Rv 7:9, 14–17; Jn 10:27–30

Today is Vocations Sunday. It is a day when we are asked to reflect on our own baptismal vocation. We all share the one baptismal vocation. The essence of that shared vocation is clearly expressed in what Jesus asks for in today's Gospel reading. He calls us to listen to his voice, the voice of the shepherd, and to follow him. These are the two characteristics that Jesus considers the most essential for those who wish to belong to him as members of his flock. In the first place we have to create the ability to listen to Jesus. We need to appreciate the life-giving quality of his word and allow it to feed our spiritual hunger and quench our spiritual thirst. Pope John XXIII said on one occasion that 'the Church is like an old village fountain and from its tap, fresh water must always flow'. The Church has the responsibility to ensure that the fresh water of Jesus' word is always flowing. We need to listen to that word and prayerfully reflect upon it. We live in a society that invades our consciousness with all kinds of images, messages, slogans and claims. We are inundated with messages and images in a way that was not true of past times to the same extent. The power and pressure of these images can be considerable. We need to make a real effort to place the living word of Jesus at the centre of our faith communities and of our own lives as believers. We need that element of silence in our lives in order to really listen to the Lord's word, especially as it comes to us in the Gospels. Pope Francis always stresses the importance of such listening, even to the extent of giving out free copies of the Gospels in St Peter's Square in the Vatican City early in his papacy. Some people find it helpful to listen to the Lord's word in the company of other believers, such as in the setting of a *Lectio Divina* prayer group.

'The sheep that belong to me listen to my voice', Jesus goes on to say, 'and they follow me.' It is not enough to listen to the Lord's voice. Our Baptism calls us to follow him as well. We have to allow his word to shape us, to mould our thoughts, words and actions. We are to believe what he believed, to give importance to what he considered important, to defend the dignity of the human person as he did, to be with the powerless and the vulnerable as he was, to be as free to do good as he was, to trust God the Father as he trusted him, to face life and death with the hope with which he faced them. The Lord calls us to allow his attitudes and values to take root in our hearts and to bear fruit in our lives, so that we can come to say with St Paul, 'It is no longer I who live but Christ who lives in me.' This is the calling we all share in virtue of our Baptism. It is such a profound and all-embracing calling that we spend our whole lives responding to it. Growing up into the person of Christ is a life's journey. It is the one journey that does full justice to our humanity. When we grow a little deaf to this calling or when we wander off from this journey, it is worth our while beginning again. The Lord continues to call, even when our response grows weak.

What Jesus goes on to say in the Gospel reading suggests that he won't let us go easily, even if we are prone to wandering off. He declares that those who belong to him 'will never be lost'. This is the confident cry of the Good Shepherd who is determined to lose nothing of what God his father has given him. The confidence of the Shepherd does not make us complacent, but it encourages us not to lose heart in times of personal failure and not to give up on ourselves, because we know that our Good Shepherd does not give up on us. Jesus' statement, 'They will never be lost', is matched by his statement, 'No one will steal them from me.' In that second statement, Jesus recognises that there are lots of forces at work in the world that would steal his followers from him. There are lots of influences in our world that seek to snatch us from the Lord. Yet, the Lord declares that his work of keeping us faithful is stronger than the forces that work to steal us from him. The Lord who calls us is also working with us, helping us to respond to his calling. Today we remind ourselves of our shared baptismal vocation and we renew our response to that calling in the confidence that, as St Paul says in his first letter to the Thessalonians (5:24), 'The one who calls you is faithful, and he will do this.'

Fifth Sunday of Easter
Jesus' new commandment to love

Acts 14:21-7; Rv 21:1-5; Jn 13:31-5

I remember when I was an altar server in my home parish, one of the priests there at the time said in a homily that as followers of Jesus we are not expected to like everyone but we are expected to love everyone. It struck a chord with me at the time. Maybe I was relieved to hear that we were not expected to like everyone; I was probably aware of several people I didn't like all that much. When we speak about liking someone, we mean that we find someone appealing or attractive; we are drawn to them in some way. They generate emotional energy in us that moves us towards them. We enjoy their company. We find it easy to love those we like and are drawn to.

In the Gospel reading Jesus calls upon us to love one another as he has loved us. He is calling for a love that goes beyond those we like. The love he is speaking about is not primarily a feeling of warmth or fondness for someone. He is speaking of a love that shows itself in action, in behaviour, even towards those for whom we feel no great fondness or affection. Jesus spoke those words just after he had washed the feet of his disciples on the night before he was crucified. Included among those whose feet Jesus washed was Judas. Judas had not yet left the room, according to the Gospel of John. Jesus was aware at this point that Judas had it in mind to betray him. Yet, he did not hesitate to get down on his knees and wash Judas' feet along with the feet of the others. Jesus must have had feelings of distress and perhaps anger in the presence of Judas and yet he acted towards him as he did towards everyone else in the room that night. Here was Jesus emptying himself in the service of someone who was about to betray him. Having washed the feet of his disciples, including Judas, Jesus then turned towards them, saying, 'I give you a new commandment:

just as I have loved you, you also must love one another.' He was calling on them, on us, to relate to one another as he had related to them, as he would relate to all men and women the following day as he hung from the cross. On the cross, Jesus was expressing God's love for everyone, including Judas, the Jewish leadership, Pilate and all who were responsible for his violent death as a criminal on a Roman cross.

This is the kind of love that can be commanded. Jesus could not command us to like everyone. We simply cannot direct and control our emotions to that extent. He can command us to love one another, in the sense of relating to one another as he relates to all of us.

Two neighbours had a nasty falling out a number of years ago. One has been trying to reach out to the other over and over again, greeting her whenever they passed one another in the street, calling out to her when she would see her in her yard, attempting, time after time, to mend the breach. Each effort on her part is rebuffed or ignored, and yet the persistent neighbour tries again and again. In many ways, these efforts exemplify the kind of love about which Jesus speaks in today's Gospel reading, which is his new commandment. You might say, 'What is new about this commandment? Doesn't the Old Testament, the Jewish Scriptures, call on us to love our neighbour as ourselves?' What is new in this commandment is the little phrase, 'just as I have loved you'. Jesus was the first human being to give full expression to God's love. His calling on us to love one another in the same divine way as he has loved us is a new commandment. Jesus also defined 'neighbour' in a new way. For Jesus, the neighbour was any and every member of the human race. We only have to think of the parable of the Good Samaritan. The broken man on the side of the road was a Jew. Yet, the Samaritan emptied himself in the service of this wounded and dying Jew, even though Jews were traditional enemies of the Samaritans. He revealed a love in action that did not discriminate. He demonstrated the kind of love that characterised the life of Jesus, a love that does not count the cost in the service of others, regardless of who they are. We need the Lord's help to love in this way, the help of the Holy Spirit. Such love is the fruit of the Spirit, in the words of St Paul.

In today's second reading, the author of the Book of Revelation has a vision of heaven coming down to earth, of God's will being done on earth as it is in heaven. He speaks of this transformed earth as the holy city, the new Jerusalem. This new city is one that begins here and now with each act that aims to fulfil Jesus' new commandment. The refusal to give up on anyone or to let another's rejection extinguish the offer of love creates a space for God to create this holy city, where all can find a home.

Sixth Sunday of Easter
A leaving that is life-giving

Acts 15:1–2, 22–9; Rv 21:10–14, 22–3; Jn 14:23–9

The experience of loss is probably one of the most difficult experiences of life. We get to know someone and grow fond of them. Then they move on from us in some way, and we find ourselves struggling to come to terms with that. The most painful experience of loss, of course, is when someone who has been hugely important to us moves on from us in death. We feel that a part of ourselves dies with them and we wonder how we will keep going without them. A heaviness of heart hangs over us and we can find it hard to rise above it. There are other experiences of loss that we have to deal with in life which are not quite as painful but nonetheless take a great deal out of us. A friendship we had great hopes for does not come to anything; a long-standing relationship breaks down. All such losses are an inevitable part of life; they cannot be avoided. We have to try and deal with them in the best way that we can, in ways that in the long run will leave us more alive rather than less alive, more willing to engage with the call of life rather than less willing.

In today's Gospel reading, Jesus is portrayed as preparing his disciples for an experience of loss that they will find devastating. The setting is the evening before Jesus is crucified, the Last Supper. Jesus says clearly to his disciples that he is going away, he is leaving them. He tries to prepare them for the crisis that his death will create for them. He tells them that his departure is in reality a good thing, because it will make it possible for him to come back to them in a new way. That is why Jesus says to his disciples not only, 'I am going away', but also, 'I am coming back'. He is leaving them in the embodied form that they have come to know and cherish, but his leaving them in this form will make it possible for him to come back to them in another form. He will come back to them through the Holy Spirit. When the Holy Spirit comes, he will make Jesus present to his disciples in a new way; he will remind them of all that Jesus has said to them; he will give them the gift of peace, the peace which comes from knowing that the Lord is powerfully present to those who love him and try to live by his word. Indeed, in today's Gospel reading, Jesus goes so far as to say that if his disciples really loved him, they would be glad that he is leaving them, because his leaving them will be life-giving not only for Jesus himself but also for all of them and for all who eventually will come to believe in Jesus. The journey that Jesus was about to undergo from this world to the Father was not the tragedy it appeared to be. It is a journey that would bear rich fruit. Without the death and Resurrection of Jesus and the sending of the Spirit that flowed from his death and Resurrection, we would not be gathered here today celebrating the presence of the Lord to us in his Word, in the Eucharist and in each other.

When we are struggling with some deep loss, it can be hard to see how anything good can come from it. At the time, all we can see is what we are losing and all we can feel is the resulting emotional pain. Yet, the words of Jesus in today's Gospel reading apply not just to the first disciples' experience of loss, the death of Jesus, but to all experiences of loss. They tell us that every experience of loss has the potential to be life-giving. The grain of wheat which falls into the ground and dies can bear much fruit, whatever form that grain of wheat takes. Those that we let go of in one form can come back to us in another form. When one particular expression of our relationship with someone dies, that relationship can find expression in new forms. Parents know that from their experience of their children. There is a letting go involved when the child first goes to school, when the young adult goes abroad for a lengthy period for the first time, or leaves the home to live more independently. There is a letting go involved when a son or daughter falls in love, gets married and starts a new home.

There is an element of real loss involved for parents in all of those experiences, and yet in the loss there is also a gain, a joy which could not be experienced without the initial pain of loss. All of us, regardless of our state in life, struggle with the experience of loss in various ways, whether it is the loss of significant others or the loss of some reality that is very important to us. The Gospel reading assures us that the pain we experience in the midst of all our losses can be the birth pangs of new life. The Advocate, the Holy Spirit, will be our helper at such times and through the Spirit, we will come to experience the Lord's peace, a peace the world cannot give.

The Ascension of the Lord
Being empowered for witness

Acts 1:1–11; Heb 9:24–8, 10:19–23; Lk 24:46–53

We have all known times of transition in our lives, when one phase of our lives comes to an end and a new phase opens up. We leave one place and move to another; we leave one job and take up a new one; we leave a group of people we have come to know and grown fond of and start to get to know a whole new group of people. It is often the way with such transitional moments that they are marked by both sadness and joy, sadness associated with the ending and joy at the prospect of a new beginning. Such moments can be difficult and unsettling, while also being exciting and energising. We struggle to let go of the familiar, while the anticipation of a new challenge draws us forward.

The Ascension of the Lord must have been such a transitional moment in the lives of Jesus' first disciples. One phase in their relationship with the Lord was coming to an end, and a new and very different phase was opening up. Jesus had been present to them in an embodied way for the best part of three years; they had been listening to his preaching; they had seen him serve people; they had walked all over Galilee with him; they had accompanied him on his journey to Jerusalem; they had shared table with him. Now all of that was coming to an end. Jesus was taking his leave of them; from now on he would no longer be visible to them in a bodily way. There was a real ending involved in Jesus' ascension. The loss and sadness associated with this is captured in today's first reading, where the disciples are described as 'staring into the sky'. Yet, this ending was at the same time a new beginning. Jesus would be present to them in another way, in and through the coming of the Holy Spirit. As he takes his leave of his disciples, he promises them, in the words of today's first reading, 'Not many days from now, you will be baptised with the Holy Spirit.' This moment of sadness was, as a result, a moment of joy as well. As Luke states in our Gospel reading, 'They went back to Jerusalem full of joy.'

If both sadness and joy characterise every experience of transition, it is the mood of joy that is much more to the fore on this feast of the Ascension. This is a joyful feast. We celebrate the new beginning in the Lord's relationship with his disciples, which his ascension made possible. When Jesus looked ahead to this moment of new beginning, he spoke in terms of power and empowerment: 'Stay in the city until you are clothed with power from on high'; 'You will receive power when the Holy Spirit comes upon you, and then you will be my witnesses'. Jesus promises his disciples that, after his departure, they will be empowered by the Holy Spirit to become his witnesses in the world. That same promise is made to disciples of every generation, to all of us gathered here today. The risen Lord empowers us through the Holy Spirit to be his witnesses in the world. The Lord's ascension opened up a new period of Spirit-empowered witness; this is the period in which all of us live; it is the period of the Church.

What is the Church, only the community of believers who witness to the Lord? There is no separation between believing and witnessing; to be a disciple of the Lord is to witness to him. There are many ways of witnessing to the Lord today. Coming together to celebrate the Eucharist on a Sunday is one of the ways we witness to the Lord. In a context in which coming to Sunday Eucharist is no longer the norm, that form of witness becomes all the more significant. From the Eucharist, we then carry our witness to the Lord into the various contexts in which we live and work. Our witness will not necessarily take the form of preaching the Gospel in a verbally explicit way; however, it will always mean living in such a way that Jesus becomes visible, audible and tangible in and through us, and his values and attitudes take flesh in us.

Whatever form our witness takes, we need to be empowered if we are to witness to the Lord. The disciples were told to first stay in the city and wait to be clothed with power from on high; there was to be a time of prayerful waiting before they went forth to witness. For us too there is always a prayerful waiting which is prior to witnessing. Indeed, it could be said that the prayerful waiting is itself a witnessing. When we wait prayerfully, we are witnessing to our dependence on the risen Lord's help. We are witnessing to our need of the Holy Spirit. Next Sunday is the feast of Pentecost. This coming week is a special time of prayerful waiting in the Church's year. We are invited today to enter into this prayerful time so that we might receive afresh the gift of the Spirit next Sunday and go forth renewed as witnesses to the Lord and all he stands for.

Pentecost Sunday
The resource of the Spirit

Acts 2:1-11; Rm 8:8-17; Jn 14:15-16, 23-6

Some of us will have had the experience of gathering around the bedside of a loved one who was dying. Time seems to stand still at such moments. Our loved one may have little to say, but whatever is said tends to be remembered. The last words of those who are near and dear to us are always treasured. I was made aware of that again by a programme on the radio recently that replayed old recordings relating to the 1916 armed rising in Dublin. Relatives of the leaders of the rising who were executed were giving their account of their last meeting with their loved ones in jail on the evening before their execution. Whatever was said on that occasion was vividly remembered and movingly relayed.

The message of Jesus to his disciples in today's Gospel reading is set within the context of the evening before he was crucified. It is the night of the Last Supper. Jesus is with his closest disciples, those who, in a sense, have been his family for the previous three years. They have travelled with him, listening to his words, observing what he was doing. Now it seems as if it is all going to end tragically. In this highly charged moment, Jesus has something important to say to these disciples. As he takes his leave of them, he promises to send them what he calls another Advocate or Paraclete. He has been their Advocate for the previous three years. Now he promises to send them another Advocate, the Holy Spirit. A Paraclete or Advocate is, literally, someone who is called to stand alongside someone else in their time of need. A Paraclete is someone you would want standing alongside you in a difficult situation. Jesus may soon be cruelly taken from his disciples but he promises that he will come to them again in and through this other Paraclete, the Holy Spirit, who is the Spirit both of Jesus himself and of God his Father.

The promise that Jesus makes to his disciples in that Gospel reading is made to all of us. The disciples who gathered around Jesus on that night before he died represent the disciples of every generation. The promise that Jesus made to his disciples came to pass for them at the Jewish feast of Pentecost, a short time after Jesus' death and Resurrection. The same promise has come to pass for us at our Baptism and Confirmation, and, indeed, every day of our lives. The risen Lord is constantly offering us the Paraclete, the Holy Spirit, to stand alongside us in our times of need, and not just to stand alongside us but to reside within us. As St Paul says in our second reading today, 'the Spirit of God has made his home in you', 'the Spirit of him who raised Jesus from the dead is living in you'. On this feast of Pentecost, we give thanks for this wonderful resource that the Lord has given to stand alongside us and to dwell within us. The readings for Pentecost remind us of some of the ways that this great gift can be a resource to us. Saint Paul in the second reading tells us that the Holy Spirit makes us cry out 'Abba, Father!' The Spirit within us inspires us to address God in the same intimate way that Jesus did, as 'Abba, Father'. The Spirit within us is always praying in this way to God. Our prayer consists of allowing ourselves to be caught up into this prayer of the Spirit which is constantly happening deep within us. Jesus makes reference to another way that the Holy Spirit is a resource for us. He says in that Gospel reading that the Holy Spirit will 'teach you everything and remind you of all I have said to you'. It is the Spirit who makes the words of Jesus preserved in the Gospels come alive for us. That is why before reading the Gospels or listening to them being read it is good to pray to the Holy Spirit. It is the Spirit who allows us to hear the Lord's word as a word for us, a word for me, here and now in the concrete circumstances of my life. The Spirit draws out new depths of meaning from the teaching of Jesus for the changing circumstances of life in which we find ourselves. Without the Spirit the Gospel would become a dead letter.

The first reading reminds us of another way that the Holy Spirit is a resource for us. On that first Pentecost the Holy Spirit empowered the disciples to communicate Jesus to others, in spite of the various language barriers. That is what the Holy Spirit does for us today. It is the Holy Spirit who empowers us to bear witness to Jesus before others, to communicate him to other by what we say and do, by who we are. The Holy Spirit is the great communicator. Today's feast is a reminder to us of the essential role of the Holy Spirit in our lives. We need to keep on praying, 'Come Holy Spirit', to keep on opening our lives more fully to this great gift of the risen Lord.

ORDINARY
TIME

The Most Holy Trinity
Called into the community of the Trinity

Prov 8:22-31; Rm 5:1-5; Jn 16:12-15

One of the distinguishing marks of Christianity, when compared with other great world religions, is belief in the Trinity. We believe that God is a community of three, without ceasing to be one. The Christian faith in Ireland was deeply Trinitarian from its origins. The prayers and writings of St Patrick show that belief in the Trinity was at the very centre of his faith. We have all been baptised in the name of the Trinity, Father, Son and Spirit. We confess our faith in the Trinity when we recite the Creed, and, more simply, when we bless ourselves.

Today's feast of the Trinity reminds us that the life of God is a community life. Within God there is a relationship of profound love between the Father, the Son, and the Holy Spirit. That community of love within God is not closed in on itself. We are all called to belong there. Saint Paul reminds us in today's second reading that the love of God, the love of the Trinity, 'has been poured into our hearts'. God the Father sent the Son and the Holy Spirit to draw us into the life of the Trinity. The Son leads us to the Father; he is the way to the Father. The Spirit, in turn, leads us to the Son. As today's Gospel reminds us, the Spirit tells us about Jesus, reminding us of all that Jesus said to us. We come to the Father, through the Son and in the Spirit. We are invited to relate to God as Father, Son and Spirit; we are called into the community of the Trinity.

Because we are made in God's image and God is a communion of love, we all long for communion with others. Even the greatest loners among us need human companionship from time to time. If we were to call to mind the happiest moments of our lives, we would probably discover that they involved some element of communion or community, some experience of a loving relationship with others.

Although, to some extent, we live in an age of great individualism, we know instinctively that we are made to be in communion with others.

Our baptismal calling is to help to create the kind of communities that in some way reflect the life of the Trinity. Whenever we are instrumental in helping to form such communities, we are doing the work of God, the work of the Trinity. The first community of love that we experience is our family. None of us have perfect families. Yet, at their best, families can be communities of love, reflections of the life of the Trinity, and each family member has a role to play in making that happen. Beyond the family, the Church is called to be a community of love. Jesus, on the night before he died, said to his disciples, 'As the Father has loved me, I have loved you ... Love one another as I have loved you.' Jesus wants the Church to be a concrete expression of the communion of love that is the Trinity. We know that the Church has frequently fallen short of this vision of Jesus. Yet, the Holy Spirit keeps on reminding us of what the Church is called to become. The parish is the local Church, and every parish is called to reflect, in some way, the loving community that is God. We can all help to make our parishes communities of love. The parish has been well described as a community of communities. There is a need for smaller communities of faith within the community of the parish, whether it is prayer groups or Scripture study groups or music groups or outreach groups.

If we look around us we will find examples of life-giving communities that are not explicitly Church related. Many adults put energy and time into bringing children together in ways that are healthy and formative. Others work to ensure that older people among us, many of whom live alone, are given opportunities to gather together in ways that are enjoyable and life-affirming. Many more put energy into creating spaces where people with special needs can gather and express themselves and share their gifts. Others offer an experience of family to those who are isolated and vulnerable. Whenever we work to make genuine community happen we are acting in a Trinitarian way. Every time we gather people together in ways that build them up as human beings, we are living in the spirit of the Trinity. That is the call and the challenge of today's feast.

Within Christianity, who God is and who we are called to be are inseparable. The Trinity is not just a theological abstraction. Trinity is a way of being. It is God's way of being and it is also to be our way of being as people who are made in God's image. Although the feast of the Trinity might initially seem remote from us, it is a very down-to-earth feast, because it reminds us of what we need to be about in our day-to-day lives. As we profess our faith in the Trinity, today, we also commit ourselves to building communities of love wherever we find ourselves.

The Body and Blood of Christ
Proclaiming the Lord's death

Gn 14:18-20; 1 Cor 11:23-6; Lk 9:11-17

Last month we celebrated the First Communion of the children in our parish. As a priest, I love celebrating a First Communion Mass. The excitement and the reverence that the children bring to that day speak to us of the great gift which is the Eucharist. Receiving this gift for the first time is a very special moment for the children. We can all learn from their appreciation of this gift. Jesus said that we need to become like little children to enter the kingdom of God. We can learn from the First Communion children to value this gift of the Eucharist which we can easily take for granted.

Today we celebrate the feast of the Eucharist, the feast of the body and blood of the Lord. In the world of Jesus, the expression 'body and blood' was a way of speaking of the whole person. 'Body' refers to the whole physical person, whereas 'blood' was understood as the life force of the person. At the Last Supper, Jesus gave his whole person, his body and blood, to his disciples under the form of bread and wine. Taking bread, he blessed it, broke it and gave it to his disciples saying, 'This is my body.' Taking a cup of wine, he blessed it and gave it to his disciples saying, 'This is the new covenant in my blood.' This self-giving of Jesus at the Last Supper under this form of bread and wine anticipated his total gift of himself to his disciples and to the world from the cross on the following day. Jesus gave himself for all of us, to all of us, on the cross, but he wanted that gift of himself to be personal to each one of us. That is why he gave himself to his disciples under the form of bread and wine at the Last Supper and told his disciples to do what he had just done in memory of him. Jesus wanted to continue giving himself, his body and blood, to his disciples of every generation. This is what happens at every Eucharist. In our second reading today,

Paul gives us the earliest account of what Jesus said and did at the Last Supper. In the time of Paul, in the decades after the death and Resurrection of Jesus, the community of believers met on a regular basis to repeat what Jesus said and did at the Last Supper. Paul refers at the end of that reading to 'every time you eat this bread and drink this cup'. 'Every time' implies that the taking, blessing, breaking and eating of the bread and the taking, blessing and drinking of the cup is happening on a regular basis. It has been happening ever since, down to our own Mass here today.

Paul declares in that reading that, whenever we eat the bread and drink the cup, we are proclaiming the Lord's death. Just as there was a very close link between the Last Supper and the death of Jesus, Paul recognises the same link between the Eucharist and the death of Jesus. Every Eucharist, like the Last Supper, proclaims the Lord's self-giving love revealed most fully in his death. In one of his letters, Paul says, 'I live by faith in the Son of God who loved me and gave himself for me.' It is that self-giving love of Jesus for each of us personally that we proclaim at every Eucharist and that is present again to each of us at every Eucharist. The Lord who gave himself to us on the cross, gives us himself, his body and blood, at the Eucharist, under the form of bread and wine. At the heart of every Eucharist is a gift, the Lord's gift of himself to us. The most appropriate response to such a gift is to receive it with thanksgiving. That is why this central ritual of the Church came to be called Eucharist, a word which derives from the Greek verb 'to give thanks'.

When Jesus said to his disciples at the Last Supper, 'Do this in remembrance of me', the 'doing' he calls for entails not just recalling and repeating his words and actions; we are also to do what those words and actions signify. We are to give expression to his self-giving love in our lives. We are to proclaim the Lord's death not just in our Eucharist but by the way we relate to each other. The Gospel reading today shows how easy it is to miss the moment when such self-giving is asked of us in the course of our lives. When the disciples became aware of the hungry crowd, they wanted to send them away. They were washing their hands of the problem. Jesus, however, wanted to give himself to the crowd; he wanted to feed their hunger himself and he wanted to involve his disciples in this service. The disciples eventually provided Jesus with the resources he needed to feed the hunger of the crowd. Even though these resources were meagre, the Lord worked powerfully through them. The Lord continues to work powerfully through our own self-giving, no matter how meagre it might seem to us. Whenever we allow the Lord to work through us in this way, we are celebrating Eucharist with our lives.

Second Sunday in Ordinary Time
The extravagance of Jesus

Is 62:1-5; 1 Cor 12:4-11; Jn 2:1-11

We have a lot of weddings here in our parish church. It is a lovely church for a wedding. I am often struck by the extent to which a couple will go to decorate the church for the wedding, especially the sanctuary area. There are often beautiful bouquets of flowers and an abundance of candles. There is an understandable extravagance about a wedding day. A couple are standing before the Lord and his Church and declaring publicly their desire and intention to love one another for better, for worse, for richer, for poorer, in sickness and in health, all the days of their lives. There is an extravagance about that kind of a promise. It is an extraordinary promise for two frail human beings to make to each other. It is a promise that has almost infinite consequences, for themselves, for the fruit of their love, their children, and for all who are part of their lives, their families and friends. A certain extravagance is understandable given the momentous nature of what is happening.

In the Gospel reading, Jesus, his mother and his disciples are present at a wedding in Cana. According to the Gospel of John, the first of the signs or miracles of Jesus takes place in the context of a wedding and the last of his signs takes place in the context of a funeral, the death of his friend Lazarus. Jesus was present to people in their times of joyful celebration and in their times of harrowing grief. The Lord is powerfully present to us in those times that engage us to the very depths of our being, times of new beginning and of significant transition. That is why many of the sacraments of the Church mark those key moments of our existence: Baptism for the moment of birth and new life; Confirmation for the moment when we pass out of childhood into adolescence; Marriage and Ordination for those moments of commitment that shape the remainder of our lives and the lives of others; the Sacrament of the Sick for the moments when we are brought face to face with our physical vulnerability, our mortality. The remaining two sacraments, Eucharist and Penance, are not so much for those special experiences of life. They are given to us for our day-to-day living. If you like, they are the sacraments of ordinary time. In the Our Father, we pray, 'Give us this day, our daily bread.' We need the bread of life, the bread of the Eucharist, on a regular basis. It is at the Eucharist that we say our personal 'yes' to the sacrament of our Baptism and invite to Lord to come to us and to grow within us. In the Our Father we also pray, 'Forgive us our trespasses, as we forgive those who trespass against us.' We are constantly in need of the Lord's mercy, and we need to regularly come before the Lord as sinners, and the privileged way we do that is through the Sacrament of Penance. Eucharist and Penance are the sacraments of ordinary time, and, yet, ordinary time is not really ordinary because it is just as much shot through with the Lord's presence as those special moments of our lives. From the perspective of faith all of time is sacred time.

Just as there tends to be an extravagance about the momentous moment when a couple give themselves to each other for life in the presence of the Lord and his Church, there was certainly something extravagant about that wedding in Cana and the source of the extravagance was Jesus. One hundred and twenty gallons of the best wine is extravagant in any culture. We can probably never recover exactly what happened at that wedding in Cana, but what we have access to is the Gospel story and the meaning that the evangelist wanted to convey to us. The Gospel reading is saying something to us about the extravagance of Jesus. He was someone who was full of God's extravagant generosity and love. Do you remember the parable of the workers in the vineyard from the Gospel of Matthew (20:1–16)? Those who worked for the last hour received the same wages as those who worked all day – extravagant in the extreme. Then there is the better-known parable where the wasteful son is welcomed home by his father and is given a great feast after shaming his family and dissipating his inheritance. More extravagance! In the opening chapter of the Gospel of John, a few verses before our Gospel reading today, the Word who became flesh is spoken of as 'full of grace and truth' and the community who stands behind this Gospel goes on to declare, 'From his fullness we have all received, grace upon grace.' We can all make that statement our own. The extravagant generosity of God in Jesus continues to grace us. According to Paul in our second reading, the 'Spirit ... distributes different gifts to different people just as he chooses.' The Spirit is at work in our lives, gracing us abundantly in ways that equip us to serve one another, just as Jesus served the married couple at Cana. At the beginning of ordinary time, we are being reminded that each day we are graced by God's extraordinary generosity so that we can be channels of God's extravagant love to each other.

Third Sunday in Ordinary Time
Jesus' mission statement

Neh 8:2-6, 8-10; 1 Cor 12:12-30; Lk 1:1-4, 4:14-21

I once watched a documentary about the Siege of Leningrad (modern-day St Petersburg), which lasted from 1941 to 1943. The population endured one of the coldest winters in living memory in 1941–2 and people died of starvation in their thousands that winter. The great Russian composer Dmitri Shostakovich composed his seventh symphony to give expression to the anguish, suffering and hopes of the Russian people and in particular the people of Leningrad. Against all the odds, in August 1942, as the city was in the midst of its siege, this great work was performed in the concert hall in Leningrad. The conductor managed to bring together the remnants of the last remaining orchestra in Leningrad. Most of them were weak and emaciated, as everyone was living on the smallest of rations. Yet, he brought an orchestra together and at the height of the siege this great work was performed before a full concert hall. Some of those who were present on that occasion are still alive and they spoke about their experience of this wonderful event. As they sat listening to the music that August of 1942, they were cold and hungry and sickly, but this wonderful musical event fed their spirits, lifted their hearts and souls, gave them a sense of their own worth and value, and strengthened them for the struggle that lay ahead.

I was reminded of that documentary by today's Gospel reading. There Jesus speaks of himself as the Spirit-filled prophet sent by God to bring good news to the poor, to proclaim liberty to captives and new sight to the blind, to set free the downtrodden and to proclaim the Lord's year of favour. The people of Leningrad during those long months of the siege were poor and captive and downtrodden; yet, at least for a short while, the performance of Shostakovich's seventh symphony was bringing good news to the poor, proclaiming liberty to captives and giving new sight to those who had been blinded by so much tragic suffering. The Lord's favour was touching these people through this beautiful creation of the human spirit, this great orchestral work. They had been experiencing the worst atrocities that human beings can inflict on other human beings. Now, in the midst of this darkness, light and hope was being brought into their lives by what was best in the human spirit, the creative genius of the composer, the tenacity of the conductor in bringing the orchestra together, the musical ability of the members of the orchestra and their determination to give of themselves even though they were weak and frail. Together they brought a glimpse of 'the year of the Lord's favour' to those who lived in darkness and in the shadow of death.

Whenever the best instincts of the human spirit find expression, something of the year of the Lord's favour becomes present in our world. When Jesus was given the scroll of the prophet Isaiah in the synagogue of Nazareth and he read a passage of his choosing, he was really making public his mission statement. He was saying to the people of his hometown, 'This is what I am about.' His Spirit-inspired mission was to give an experience of God's favour to those who were most in need of it: the poor, both the materially poor or the spiritually poor; the captives, enslaved by their economic circumstances or by a way of life that was contrary to God's will for them; the blind, both the physically blind or the spiritually blind. This remains Jesus' mission today. He wishes to continue to proclaim this year of God's favour through us, his followers.

In today's second reading, Paul speaks about the community of the Lord's followers, the Church, as the body of Christ. All of us together are now Christ's body in the world. The Spirit of the Lord that empowered and directed Jesus' mission has been given to us, the members of Christ's body. As Paul says at the beginning of that second reading, 'In the one Spirit we were all baptised, Jews as well as Greeks, slaves as well as free, and one Spirit was given to us all to drink.' The Spirit of the Lord can bring what is best in our human spirit to full expression, and whenever that happens the poor experience good news and those who are captive discover a new freedom. Paul reminds us in that reading that there is great diversity in the body of Christ. We each have different gifts of nature which the Spirit of God can bring fully to life. Like an orchestra, we each have a unique contribution to make to the Lord's mission in today's world. The gifts of each one of us are needed and each of us needs the gifts of everyone else. The Lord looks to each of us to place our gifts and our energies at his disposal, at the disposal of the Holy Spirit, so that he can continue to proclaim the year of the Lord's favour in our world today.

Fourth Sunday in Ordinary Time
The call to a divine love

Jer 1:4-5, 17-19; 1 Cor 12:31-13:13; Lk 4:21-30

It is probably true to say that the most common theme of modern songs is that of love, the romantic love between two people. The same is probably true of most films. If romantic love is not the main plot, it will be a significant subplot. None of this is surprising. The romantic attraction between people generates great energy and easily gives rise to drama. In today's second reading we find Paul's great hymn to love. It is often chosen as one of the readings at a wedding Mass. People who are getting married recognise that there is a vision of love here that is worth aspiring to, an ideal of love that is attractive.

In that passage, Paul is not primarily giving a picture or portrait of what we would understand as romantic love. It is more the kind of love that can often be found between people who have been together for a while and who have learned what authentic love means through sometimes painful experience. It has been said that the kind of love Paul is describing here is more like a divine love than a human love. It is almost as if he is giving us a portrait of God's love in human form. As Christians, we recognise the person of Jesus to be the fullest expression of God's love in human form. In that sense, Paul's portrait of love is really a portrait of Jesus, and if the word 'Jesus' was substituted for the word 'love' the passage would read very well. Jesus is always patient and kind, is never jealous or boastful or conceited, is never rude of selfish. He does not take offence and is not resentful; he takes no pleasure in other people's sins. He delights in the truth, and is always ready to excuse, to trust, to hope and to endure whatever comes. He does not come to an end.

We could ask ourselves, 'Well, if this is a description of Jesus, in what sense could it ever be a description of my life?' Yet, clearly Paul believed that what he wrote about love was hugely relevant to the people he was writing to, the Church in Corinth, and, therefore, by implication, to us all. He begins that passage by saying, 'I am going to show you a way that is better than any of them.' Here is the way, he is saying, that we are all called to walk. He goes so far as to say that unless we are on this particular road, all the gifts we possess are worth nothing. Indeed, he goes even further and declares, 'Without love, I am nothing at all.' Paul seems to be saying that to the extent that we are at least reaching towards this kind of love, then our lives, as human beings, will be worthwhile. There is an ideal of love here that none of us can attain all the time. How many of us are always patient and kind, always delighting in the truth, always ready to excuse? How many of us are never boastful or conceited, never rude or selfish, never take offence, are never resentful, never take pleasure in others' sins? We might think to ourselves, 'This is too far beyond me.' Yet, Paul puts this ideal of love before us not to make us feel badly about how far short of it we fall, but rather to give us something worthwhile to strive for. Paul would say that we need the help of the Holy Spirit to love in this way. His description of love here is very similar to what he calls the 'fruit of the Spirit' in another of his letters. If we are to love in this divine way, we need a divine help, the Holy Spirit who helps us in our weakness. I like that prayer which is very much embedded in our Catholic tradition, 'Come Holy Spirit, fill my heart and kindle in me the fire of your love.' This is one of the prayers that children preparing of Confirmation are taught. It is a good prayer to hang on to, not just as children but into adulthood.

In today's Gospel reading the people of Nazareth take offence at Jesus. They were enraged by him. They fail to show the love towards Jesus that Paul talks about, the love that does not take offence and that is never resentful. They were enraged at Jesus' very generous vision of God, a God who was as much concerned about widows in Sidon and lepers in Syria as about widows and lepers in Israel. There was something very narrowly focused about the people of Nazareth's love. They loved the members of their own tribe but had little regard for those beyond it, those who were different, who were other. This is not the divine love that Jesus embodies. In response to the angry rejection of him by the people of Nazareth, we are told that 'he slipped through the crowd and walked away'. In the words of Paul, he did not take offence and was not resentful; he endured what came his way as a result of his preaching of the Gospel. This is the love to which we are all called and which is possible for us all through the power of the Spirit.

Fifth Sunday in Ordinary Time

The Lord touching our lives

Is 6:1–8; 1 Cor 15:1–11; Lk 5:1–11

A person's faith journey is very personal and, indeed, unique to each individual. There can come a time in our lives when the journey of faith seems almost to disappear. What had been a clearly visible path can become very faint; our faith seems to grow very week. For some people there can then come a time of spiritual reawakening. They rediscover their faith. Having drifted from the community of faith, they begin to feel a call to return to it. There can be many factors in a person's life that can contribute to such a reawakening. Sometimes children have a way of reawakening the faith of their parents. When the time comes for children to be baptised or to make their First Communion or their Confirmation, parents can feel a call to reflect anew on their own faith. Some painful experience in our lives, such as the onset of serious illness in ourselves or our loved ones, can also be a moment of spiritual reawakening. The witness of someone else's faith can touch us in some deep way and reawaken our own dormant faith. We might find ourselves at some liturgical celebration, such as the funeral Mass of a friend, where we have an experience of the Lord's presence that somehow calls us to a renewal of our faith. These experiences of spiritual reawakening tend to be very ordinary and non-dramatic for most people. A seed is sown and it grows very gradually. For some people, such experiences can be more dramatic. They experience a sudden reawakening of their faith.

Each of the three readings for this Sunday describes a moment of spiritual reawakening. While the three experiences have a great deal in common, each one is quite distinctive. In the first reading, Isaiah of Jerusalem has a moment of spiritual reawakening in a setting of worship, while in the most sacred place for the people of Israel, the temple in Jerusalem. Isaiah had a sense of the Lord's presence filling not just the temple but the whole earth, 'Heaven and earth are full of your glory.' In the second reading, Paul speaks of his moment of spiritual reawakening while he was on the main road from Jerusalem to Damascus, close to the city of Damascus. He was engaged in what he considered at the time to be God's work, persecuting the followers of Jesus. Suddenly the very Jesus whose followers he was persecuting appeared to him, 'Last of all, he appeared to me too.' In the Gospel reading, Simon Peter had a moment of spiritual reawakening, an experience of the powerful presence of the Lord, on the Sea of Galilee, while he was working at his trade as a fisherman. These were three very different people, Isaiah, Paul and Simon Peter, and the Lord touched their lives in a way that was unique to each one of them. The Lord met them where they were and spoke to them in a way that was best suited to their own situation in life.

The Lord speaks to us too in and through our own unique experience of life. Some of us may have the strongest sense of the Lord's presence when we are in a sacred place, like Isaiah. Yet, Paul and Simon Peter's experience of the Lord as they went about their daily chores reminds us that the Lord does not confine himself to our sacred places. In the Gospels there are other examples of people having a spiritual awakening in and through the ordinary experiences of their lives. The two disciples on the road to Emmaus encountered the Lord in a fellow traveller, although it took them a while to recognise him. The Lord often comes to us in and through the routine circumstances of our lives; it is above all there that we can be powerfully touched by his presence. The readings today also suggest that a significant spiritual experience is not the prerogative of some kind of spiritual elite. At the very moment when Isaiah, Simon Peter and Paul were overwhelmed by a sense of the Lord's presence, they had a strong awareness of themselves as sinners. Isaiah cried out, 'I am a man of unclean lips and

I live among a people of unclean lips.' Peter exclaimed to Jesus, 'Leave me Lord; I am a sinful man.' Looking back at his moment of spiritual reawakening, Paul acknowledges that at the time he was 'persecuting the church of God'. That is why he states publicly, 'I hardly deserve the name apostle.' The Lord does not wait for us to be worthy to disclose his presence to us or to touch our lives in some significant way. All that is needed is for us to have an openness of heart and spirit to his presence.

When we experience a spiritual reawakening it is never just for ourselves. When the Lord touches our lives in some deep way it is always for the sake of others; there will be some kind of a sending involved. Isaiah was sent to the people of Jerusalem, Simon Peter was sent to his fellow Jews and Paul was sent to the Gentiles. For most of us, the people to whom we will be sent will be those among whom we live and work, with whom we have daily contact. An experience of spiritual reawakening is always both a gift to us and a gift for others.

Sixth Sunday in Ordinary Time
Timely words

Jer 17:5–8; 1 Cor 15:12, 16–20; Lk 6:17, 20–6

In the course of our lives we invariably find ourselves speaking in different ways to different people. We might speak comforting words to those who are struggling; we can speak challenging words to those we have some responsibility for and who are not measuring up. Understanding what it is that needs to be said for the good of the other person at any particular time is a great gift.

What is true of all of us as human beings was certainly true of Jesus. He spoke different sets of words to different people. The Gospels suggest that he had mastered the art of knowing what to say and when to say it. He could find the words that people needed to hear, and he was aware that different kinds of people needed to hear different kinds of words. We have a good example of that in today's Gospel reading. Jesus addresses words of comfort to the poor, the hungry, those who weep and the persecuted. He addresses words of warning to the rich, the self-satisfied, those who were used to the adulation of others. The most vulnerable, who had least in terms of human supports and human prospects, needed to hear words of comfort. They need to be assured that, whatever about anybody else, God had certainly not forgotten them, and that a day would come when the totally unacceptable situation in which they found themselves would be reversed, 'You shall be satisfied; you shall laugh.' For some of this group, such as Lazarus in the parable that Jesus speaks later on in Luke's Gospel, the reversal would happen only beyond this life. Yet, in speaking that parable, Jesus was making clear that Lazarus should not have had to wait that long for his situation to be reversed. If others had been sufficiently generous with their resources, Lazarus' situation could have been reversed long before he died.

If the most vulnerable needed to hear words of comfort, Jesus was equally clear that the complacent rich needed to hear words of warning. In today's Gospel reading Jesus addresses challenging words to the self-satisfied rich people of his day who had totally isolated themselves from the vast bulk of the population that were living at subsistence level. Jesus painted an unforgettable picture of such a self-satisfied rich person in another parable of Luke's Gospel, what is often termed the parable of the rich fool. The man in that parable had more of this world's goods than he knew what to do with, and his only preoccupation was where to store it all. He saw his surplus as a problem to be solved rather than as a bonus that carried social responsibilities. Jesus knew that it was precisely this self-serving attitude on the part of a minority in his society that resulted in the vast bulk of the population living such vulnerable and miserable lives.

We cannot, of course, equate the society in which we are living today with the peasant society of Galilee in which Jesus preached the Gospel. For one thing, there was no concept of a social welfare state in the time of Jesus and his contemporaries. Yet, it is as true today as it was in Jesus' time that the message of the Gospel that Jesus preached has something of the quality of a two-edged sword. At times the Gospel message will find expression in words of comfort; at other times it will come to expression in words that are very challenging. To reduce the message of the Gospel to reassuring words of comfort alone is to distort it; likewise, to reduce it to a disturbing word of challenge is equally to distort it. The beatitudes and the woes that Jesus speaks in our Gospel reading today are both integral to the Gospel message, and both sets of words can be addressed to all of us at different times.

There are times in the course of our life's journey when we need to hear the Lord's assurance that when we are at our most vulnerable, he will be there for us. They are times when we desperately need to know that when everything has been taken from us, whether it is our health, our wealth, our good name, our independence, the Lord is the one reality that cannot be taken from us, because he is especially close to the broken-hearted, to those whose spirits are crushed. He has come as strength in our weakness, as life in our various deaths, and those who keep on trusting in him in spite of everything are like trees whose foliage stays green when the heat comes, in the image of today's first reading.

There are other times in our lives when we need to hear the challenging and tough side of the Lord's Gospel message. We can all get complacent. We can easily imagine that all is well with our little world, when, in reality, what we are doing, and sometimes what we are failing to do, is having damaging consequences for others. There are times when, in our dullness of spirit, we desperately need to hear the Lord's wake-up call. All of the Lord's words, both the challenging ones and the comforting ones, are spoken in love and their purpose is to show us the path of life for ourselves and for others. This Sunday we commit ourselves anew to listening and taking to heart all of his words.

Seventh Sunday in Ordinary Time
Overcoming evil with good

1 Sm 26:2, 7–9, 12–13, 22–3; 1 Cor 15:45–9; Lk 6:27–38

Some time ago, I was watching a television programme on the genocide that happened in Rwanda in 1994. Savagery ensued when one tribe, the Hutu, turned on the members of another tribe, the Tutsi, and hundreds of thousands of people were murdered. The United Nations pulled out most of its troops just as the genocide was unfolding. The television programme focused on Canadian general Roméo Dallaire, who stayed with a very small force during the genocide and tried to do what he could for the people of Rwanda, until he could take no more and asked to be relieved of his post. He wrote a book entitled *Shake Hands with the Devil*. He gave the book this title because he felt that whenever he encountered those who were carrying out this atrocity, he had a sense that he was in touch with the devil in human form. He went on to say that in the midst of all that unmitigated evil, he also came across great goodness, and that, if the devil was at work in that situation, so also God was at work. It was obvious from watching the programme that he himself was one expression of such goodness.

There are many moments in human history when sheer evil shows its ugly face in a very shocking fashion. Still within living memory for many people, the attempted extermination of the Jewish people by the Nazis comes to mind. These are manifestations of evil on a massive scale that leave us perplexed and confused. We find ourselves asking how human beings could do such things to other human beings. We are all aware of manifestations of evil closer to home on a smaller scale. We hear about them every week on our radios and televisions. We read about them in our newspapers. A man walks into another man's home and shoots him dead in front of his partner and children. We wonder how one human being could do that to another human being.

What do we do when faced with evil, whether it is on a grand or a small scale? Jesus was addressing those questions in today's Gospel reading. Although Jesus was someone who knew the good that we are all capable of and who called people to aspire to that goodness, he was also a realist. He knew the evil that human beings were capable of. He knew the damage they could do to each other. He knew what would be done to him because of the message that he proclaimed and the life that he lived. In today's Gospel reading, then, he refers to 'those who hate you', 'those who curse you', 'those who treat you badly'.

The people that Jesus was speaking to were familiar with the second of the two great commandments, 'Love your neighbour as yourself.' Jesus went much further than this commandment, calling on people to love their enemies, to do good to those who hated them. If this went beyond the teaching of the Jewish law, it certainly went beyond the whole ethos of the culture of the time. Most people would have considered this teaching folly in the extreme. Doing good to those who did good to you was the most that could be expected of anybody.

The teaching of Jesus in the Gospel reading retains something of its power to shock, even today. Saint Paul in his letter to the Romans captured the essence of Jesus' teaching when he called on them, 'Do not be overcome by evil, but overcome evil with good.' We are only too well aware of the ways that evil can generate evil. We probably only have to look into our own hearts and lives to see how easily this can happen. Someone treats us badly and we feel a strong impulse to react accordingly. Those who treat us badly can bring out the worst in us. It is not without good reasons that people speak of a cycle of violence, of tit-for-tat killings.

The world desperately needs people who can overcome evil with good, who do not allow the goodness that is within them to be taken from them by evil. Jesus in the Gospel reading today makes clear that for those who claim to be his disciples, doing good only to those who do good to them is not enough. He calls us to live as sons and daughters of the God who is kind to the ungrateful and the wicked. Jesus revealed this God more than any other human being ever could. He prayed for those who crucified him; he continued to offer the Gospel to those who, like the Samaritans, initially rejected him. He was what Paul calls in the second reading, the heavenly man. Paul reminds us in that reading that we are all destined to become that heavenly person, to be conformed to the image of God's son. The Lord in today's Gospel calls on us to begin to live now in accordance with the person we are destined to become. We can only do this with his help, in the power of the Holy Spirit whom the Lord continues to pour out on all who know their need of this gift.

Eighth Sunday in Ordinary Time
Words from a good heart

Sir 27:4-7; 1 Cor 15:54-8; Lk 6:39-45

There are several references to trees and the fruit that they bear in today's readings. The first reading from one of the Wisdom books of the Jewish Scriptures declares that the orchard where the tree grows is judged on the quality of its fruit. The responsorial psalm speaks of palm trees and Lebanon cedars that still bear fruit when they are old. In the Gospel reading, Jesus declares that the nature of every tree can be told by its own fruit. In each of these three instances, the reference is not primarily to trees and their fruit as to people and their qualities.

Jesus declares that just as good fruit reveals that the tree it came from is sound or healthy, so the goodness that someone displays by their words and deeds reveals that their 'heart' is sound and healthy, or, in the words of the Gospel reading, that their heart contains a store of goodness. When Jesus speaks of 'heart' here, he is speaking about the person's inner core, the deepest part of their being. If our inner core is good, it will be visible in what we say and do. In the very last sentence of the Gospel reading, Jesus highlights, in particular, how the words we speak reveal the quality of that inner core, 'A person's words flow out of what fills their heart.' Or in another translation, 'It is out of the abundance of the heart that the mouth speaks.' We can all be good a hiding our true selves from others, and even from ourselves, but, sooner or later, our speech gives us away. I know from my own experience that when I speak to someone in a way that leaves a lot to be desired, there is something not quite right with my 'heart', that deep centre from which all else springs. I become aware that I have some 'heart work' to do. If a person's words flow out of what fills his or her heart, as Jesus says in today's Gospel reading, then, when my speech is off kilter, my heart is not filled in the way the Lord would want.

Earlier in the Gospel reading, Jesus gave an example of speech that is off kilter, that leaves a lot to be desired. Someone offers to put another right, 'Let me take out the splinter that is in your eye', while being gloriously oblivious to the plank in their own eye. Here is a case of the blind trying to lead the blind. There is no shortage of examples of that kind of speech all around us, where those who seem to have little or no self-critical sense wax eloquent in their criticism of others. We can all be prone to it, to varying degrees. Jesus would consider such speech as an example of bad fruit. We need to watch our speaking because it can be very revealing of where our heart is at that moment. The remarks of Jesus in the Gospel reading echo those of the author of the first reading from the book of Ecclesiasticus, which was written a little over a hundred and fifty years before Jesus was born. In that reading, the writer declares that a 'person's words betray what he (or she) feels' and that how someone speaks is the real test of the person. We often say that actions speak louder than words, and, yet, the words we speak are themselves actions, and some of our most influential actions are the words that we say. Harmful words can cause as much distress to someone as harmful actions. Wounds from words do not heal so easily. History has shown more than once that the harmful words spoken by political leaders can inspire great numbers of people to do harmful actions. Those who wish to dominate others are generally only too well aware of the power of propaganda.

As people of faith, we appreciate that great care is needed in speaking. As followers of the Word, who was with God in the beginning, and who is God, and who became flesh, we are very attentive to the quality of our words. We know that how we speak is a good indication of what is happening in our hearts. Jesus, the Word of God, revealed the heart of God when he spoke. As followers of the incarnate Word, we are all called to reveal something of the heart of God in the way we speak. The Lord wants to take up residence in our heart, so that we can come to say with St Paul, 'It is no longer I who live but it is Christ who lives in me.' Insofar as we allow the Lord to dwell in our deepest core, then the words that we speak will have something of the quality of the Word who became flesh and lived among us. As people of faith, we are to stand out by our refusal to speak ill of others even when goaded to do so. This does not mean that people of faith cannot call a spade a spade when that is called for. Perhaps St Paul has expressed what is required of us when it comes to speech better than any other writer in the New Testament, 'Speaking the truth in love, we must grow up in every way into him who is the head, into Christ.'

Ninth Sunday in Ordinary Time
The faith of the outsider

1 Kgs 8:41–3; Gal 1:1–2, 6–10; Lk 7:1–10

People can often surprise us in ways that encourage us and build us up. We can find ourselves astonished at someone's generosity of spirit, especially when we might not have been expecting it. We might be astonished at someone's courageous witness to their faith in a hostile environment or at the lengths to which someone goes to support and nurture a seriously ill friend. Those experiences can restore our faith in humanity. It is good to retain our capacity to be astonished by the unexpected ways that the Lord's grace can show itself in the lives of others.

The one person above all others whose goodness, generosity of spirit, courage and self-emptying love left others astonished was Jesus. The Gospels often make reference to people being astonished at Jesus, either at what he says or what he does. In today's Gospel reading, however, it is Jesus who is described as being astonished at someone. This is the only instance where the evangelist Luke in his Gospel attributes astonishment to Jesus. He is astonished at the quality of faith in him shown by a Roman centurion, a pagan, a member of the occupying power. 'I tell you', Jesus says, 'not even in Israel have I found faith like this.' The faith of this outsider to the Jewish world shows itself in a number of striking ways. He is determined to do all he can to restore his servant's health. Although a pagan, he clearly had great sensitivity towards the Jewish community. It was a group of Jewish elders that he sent to Jesus, a Jew, with his request for Jesus to heal his servant. Indeed, according to those same Jewish elders, this centurion had financed the building of the local synagogue in Capernaum. He clearly was someone capable of building bridges between different social and religious groups. When the centurion heard that Jesus was approaching his house in response to his plea, he sent another delegation to Jesus, this time a group of his own friends. If the message he gave the first group of intermediaries related to his seriously ill servant, the message he gave this second group of intermediaries related more to himself, 'Sir, I am not worthy to have you under my roof … give the word and let my servant be cured.' He thereby displayed great awareness around the sensitivities of a Jewish prophet like Jesus entering a pagan household like his own. He also showed tremendous trust in the healing power of Jesus' word. The centurion was a man of authority, but he recognises in Jesus an authority over life and death that is much greater than his own authority.

There are elements of the centurion's faith which are instructive for us today, such as his humility in recognising his unworthiness to have Jesus come to his home. As a Roman centurion, he was a person of some status and influence. Yet, he recognised that Jesus was his superior. We all need to come before the Lord in that same spirit of humility, recognising our unworthiness before him. We always approach the Lord as sinners before one who is all good and all loving. The only way to God is the way of humility, simplicity and transparency. God is always greater than us, and we come before God recognising our limitations. Yet, this recognition of our unworthiness before the Lord does not cause us to keep our distance from him. This brings us to another element of the centurion's faith, his profound trust in the healing and life-giving power of the Lord's word, 'Give the word …' In coming before the Lord in our unworthiness, we too, at the same time, recognise his healing and life-giving word. In coming before the Lord in our weakness, we recognise that he can give us his strength. In coming before him in our sinfulness, we are aware that he will not hesitate to give us his mercy. In coming before him in our brokenness, we know that he will bring us healing.

It is striking that the Church places a version of the centurion's words on our lips at every Eucharist. We make his faith our own when we say, 'Lord, I am not worthy to have you under my roof. Say but the word and my soul will be healed.' As we approach the Eucharist, we are aware of our unworthiness to receive this gift. We come to the Eucharist as people who tire and stumble on the pilgrimage of life. Yet, this sense of our unworthiness does not keep us away from the Eucharist because, like the centurion, we have a balancing confidence in the healing and life-giving power of the Lord's word. We know that we don't deserve this wonderful gift, but we also know that the Lord does not ask us to deserve it. Rather, he desires us to receive this unmerited gift of his self-giving love. The Lord wants to grace us in his love and our only response can be one of thanksgiving. When the Eucharist is received in this way, it nourishes our faith and inspires our living of our faith. We go forth from the Eucharist ready to grace others in the way we have been graced, just as the centurion in today's Gospel seems to have graced so many people by his goodness and generosity of spirit.

Tenth Sunday in Ordinary Time
Life-giving compassion

1 Kgs 17:17–24; Gal 1:11–19; Lk 7:11–17

There is perhaps no greater sadness than for a parent to have to bury a son or a daughter. As children, we expect our parents to die before us. Parents, likewise, do not expect their children to die before them. The death of a young person before his or her parent seems a reversal of human expectations. A very intense sadness hangs over such a funeral. Both today's first reading and Gospel reading put before us the deep grief of a mother at the death of her child.

At the beginning of the Gospel reading, a parade of life meets with a parade of death. Jesus accompanied by his disciples and a great number of people approach the gate of the town of Nain. Coming in the opposite direction is a dead man being carried out for burial, the only son of his widowed mother who walks alongside her son's bier, surrounded by a considerable number of the people of Nain. When these two very different processions meet, something extraordinary happens. Without waiting to be asked to do anything, Jesus restores life to the young man and gives him back to his mother. As a result, the parade of death becomes a parade of joy with people filled with awe and praising God. The Gospel reading reminds us that Jesus has entered our world as a life-giver. In the words of the great prayer of Zechariah, the father of John the Baptist, Jesus reveals the tender mercy of God by giving light to those who sit in darkness and in the shadow of death. Jesus was close to people in their grief. He stood alongside Mary and Martha whose brother Lazarus had just died and brought life out of their experience of death. The same risen Lord stands among us as light in our darkness and as life in our death. Whenever we find ourselves as part of some parade of death, we can be assured that the Lord of life is drawing near to us. He comes to bring us life so that we in turn can be his messengers of life to others.

In the time of Jesus, widows were considered very vulnerable; they no longer had their main provider, their husband. Widows often had to depend on their children, particularly their sons, to support them. A widow who lost her only son through death was, therefore, the most vulnerable of all. It is said of Jesus in today's Gospel reading that when he saw the grieving widow he had compassion for her. In two of the parables that Jesus speaks in Luke's Gospel, we find that same description of a compassionate response to someone in need. The Samaritan had compassion for the broken traveller and the father had compassion for his returning son, just as Jesus had compassion for the widow. The compassion shown by the Samaritan, by the father and by Jesus is a revelation of God's compassionate love for the broken.

It is not said of the widow in today's Gospel reading that she had faith or that she asked Jesus for anything. Jesus simply reaches out to her in her need. Compassion does not ask questions about a person's suitability to be served. Jesus, the Samaritan and the father all acted out of compassion without waiting to be asked, without asking questions or making a judgement as to whether the person was deserving of help or not. Jesus is often portrayed as responding to people's faith, but he is also portrayed as taking the initiative towards people without asking after their faith. This might be reassuring to remember when our own faith seems weak. The Gospel reminds us that the Lord's initiative in our regard is not dependant on our having a certain level of faith. He comes towards us as we are, and the greater our need, the stronger his coming. The Lord graces us with his presence and his gifts. Having been surprisingly and undeservedly graced by the Lord's compassionate presence, we cannot but respond to such a grace in the way that the crowd did in today's Gospel reading, 'Everyone was filled with awe and praised God, saying "A great prophet has appeared among us; God has visited his people."'

As followers of Jesus, we too recognise that God was visiting us in and through the ministry of Jesus. We also recognise that God continues to visit today in and through his Son, now risen Lord. Paul, the great persecutor of the Church, came to this conviction through a life-changing experience he had just outside the city of Damascus. In today's second reading, Paul reflects on that moment, declaring, 'God, who had specially chosen me while I was still in my mother's womb, called me through his grace and chose to reveal his son in me'. Paul came to understand in that moment that God was visiting him through Jesus, God's son, risen from the dead. God continues to visit us all through his risen son, even if not in the same dramatic way. We need to stand ready for those moments of divine visitation, because they will come our way, even when we are not seeking them. As in the case of Paul, those moments when God visits us through his son will be both moments of grace and moments of call. In gracing us, God will be calling us to become life-givers through our compassionate presence to others, in the way Jesus was.

Eleventh Sunday in Ordinary Time
The quality of gratitude

2 Sm 12:7–10, 13; Gal 2:16, 19–21; Lk 7:36–8:3

When we reflect on our lives, we can sometimes become very aware of what is lacking. We look at others and in comparison to them we conclude that we are not as fortunate. They may be healthier than we are or more prosperous or whatever. Yet, we can easily miss the many ways that we ourselves have been blessed, the many reasons that we have for giving thanks. Gratitude to God has always been at the heart of what it means to be a follower of the Lord. God has greatly blessed all of us in and through his son. Like Paul in today's second reading, we can all say, 'I live by faith in the son of God who loved me and sacrificed himself for my sake.' We too have much to give thanks for.

The word 'Eucharist' comes from the Greek word 'to give thanks'. The Eucharist is our great act of thanksgiving. We give thanks to God, through Christ, in the Spirit, for the many ways God has blessed and continues to bless us through the life, death and Resurrection of Jesus. To that extent, our regular celebration of the Eucharist helps to keep us grateful people. At the Eucharist, we recognise together that we have been greatly graced by the Lord and we respond by giving thanks.

Today's Gospel reading puts before us someone who demonstrates in a very dramatic way that quality of gratitude to God. The woman's lavish service of the Lord in the house of Simon the Pharisee was the outpouring of a grateful heart. Sometime in the recent past, she had an overwhelming experience of being graced by God, through the person of Jesus. She came to the realisation, through her encounter with him, that she was greatly loved by God and abundantly forgiven. Having experienced God's merciful love through the person of Jesus, she wanted to give expression to the love she had received in a loving way. Without waiting to be invited, she broke into a meal at which Jesus was a guest and, in a most unselfconscious manner, she showed her gratitude for the love and mercy she had received. This was her Eucharist, her great act of thanksgiving to God, through Christ. She shows us what gratitude looks like in practice: it is bold and spontaneous and it does not count the cost.

The woman was so grateful to Jesus because she was aware of how much she had received from him. The host at that meal, Simon, was not grateful to Jesus because he had no sense that he had anything to receive from Jesus. As a Pharisee, Simon thought of himself as someone who kept God's law, whereas he clearly had doubts about Jesus' reputation as a prophet. Those who think they have nothing to receive from others have no reason to be grateful to them. If Simon thought he had nothing to receive from Jesus, he was very clearly of the view that he had even less to receive from the woman who barged into his meal uninvited. If Jesus had a dubious reputation as a prophet, in Simon's eyes the woman had a well-earned reputation as a sinner. Yet, the reality was that Simon had a great deal to receive from both Jesus and the woman. Jesus, in fact, points to the woman as someone who has something to teach Simon. He had much to learn from her about the art of showing hospitality, if nothing else. That is why Jesus asked him, 'Simon, you see this woman?' He was inviting Simon to see her with new eyes.

At the root of all gratitude is the recognition that we have a great deal to receive from others and a willingness to receive from them. We go through life as beggars, as learners. At every moment of our lives, we stand before others as people who always have more to receive than to give. If this is true of our relationship with others, it is even truer of our relationship with the Lord. We stand before him as people in need. We are in need of his mercy, his grace, his strength, his wisdom, his Spirit. In his presence we recognise our poverty, our weakness. Out of that recognition, we are open to receive from his fullness. We look to him to grace us. In practice, it is often through others that the Lord is most likely to grace us. We have a great deal to receive from the Lord present in each other. We often have most to receive from those who may appear to have least to give us, just as Simon had most to learn from the woman he considered had nothing to teach him.

Jesus once said, 'Whoever does not receive the kingdom of God as a little child will never enter it.' We need a child-like openness to receive what God is always offering us through those among whom we live and work. If we have such openness, the Lord will grace us in ways that will surprise us, and, in response, our lives will become one great act of thanksgiving. We will become eucharistic people who, in the words of St Paul, 'Give thanks in all circumstances.'

Twelfth Sunday in Ordinary Time
Coming to know Jesus

Zec 12:10–11, 13:1; Gal 3:26–9; Lk 9:18–24

We probably have an average of seven or eight Baptisms per month in our parish. They are always very joyful events. The babies are at the centre of the celebration; we all gather around them in a spirit of wonder and gratitude. Immediately after the moment of Baptism at the font, the mother or the godmother is asked to wrap the white baptismal shawl around the child. Addressing the children who have just been baptised, the celebrant says, 'You have been clothed with Christ. See in this white garment the outward sign of your Christian dignity.' The clothing of the baptised with a white garment has been part of the baptismal liturgy since the earliest days of the Church. This little ritual was probably inspired by what Paul says about Baptism in today's second reading, 'All baptised in Christ, you have all clothed yourselves in Christ'. Paul understood that because of Baptism, Christ enfolds us, embraces us. The well-known prayer that is associated with St Patrick, St Patrick's breastplate, captures very well that sense of being enfolded by Christ through Baptism: Christ within me, Christ behind me, Christ before me, Christ beside me, Christ beneath me, Christ above me.

Paul goes on to state in that reading that because, through Baptism, we are all enfolded by Christ, there is a fundamental equality and unity between all the baptised, regardless of race, social status or gender. 'There are no more distinctions', he says, 'between Jew and Greek, slave and free, male and female, but all of you are one in Christ Jesus.' Because through baptism we have all clothed ourselves in Christ, we are all brothers and sisters in Christ. We are all members of one family of believers, and within that family there are no distinctions. We may have different callings and different roles within the Church, but fundamentally we are equal and we are one. Christ is equally close to every one of us. He is as close to us as we are to ourselves, even though we may not always be aware of his presence.

We all have people in our lives who are close to us, and to whom we are close. We know those people best of all. Yet, we are very aware that even those who are closest to us remain something of a mystery. We may think we know someone we are close to very well, and then we discover that there was something significant going on in their lives that we knew nothing about. Getting to know even those who are closest to us is the journey of a lifetime. Indeed, getting to know ourselves is a lifetime's work. How much more so, then, is getting to know someone else?

Our Baptism calls us to get to know Christ, the one into whom we are baptised, the one who envelopes us and surrounds us, who is within us and behind us, before us and beside us, beneath us and above us. We are called to know him not just with our head but with our heart; we are called to that knowledge which is the fruit of love. Coming to know Christ in this way is certainly a lifetime's work. We will never know him fully in this life, of course. As St Paul says in his first letter to the Corinthians, 'Now I know only in part, then (in the next life) I will know fully, even as I have been fully known.' Yet, in this life we are called to keep on growing in our knowledge of Christ, in our relationship with him. This growth in our relationship with Christ is one of the great adventures of faith that we take on at the time of our Baptism.

At any particular moment of that faith journey, the Lord could put to us the question that he puts to his disciples in today's Gospel reading, 'Who do you say I am?' That question is not primarily theoretical. He is not saying, 'Tell me everything you know about me.' It is a much more personal question. He is asking, 'Who am I for you? What significance do I have in your life?' Are you as close to me as I am to you? Am I significant enough for you to walk in my way, to live by my values, even though it might mean the cross, even though it will mean dying to self so as to live more fully to others? Peter's answer to the question of Jesus, 'You are the Christ of God', was true in so far as it went; however, events would show that Jesus was not sufficiently significant to Peter for him to remain faithful to Jesus when that involved the way of the cross. Peter was prepared to deny Jesus in order to protect himself. To that extent, in spite of his fine words, Peter was not as close to Jesus as he thought. We all have sympathy for Peter because we see ourselves in him. Peter's experience reminds us that no matter where we are in our relationship with Jesus, we are always only on the way towards giving an adequate answer to Jesus' question, 'Who do you say I am?'

Thirteenth Sunday in Ordinary Time
Responding to rejection

1 Kgs 19:16, 19–21; Gal 5:1, 13–18; Lk 9:51–62

We have all had experiences of rejection in the course of our lives. Sometimes the rejection is small enough. Perhaps we put forward some suggestion or proposal that we are committed to and it is not accepted. Such experiences are relatively easy to live with. We can also have experiences of rejection that are a lot more wounding. Some person we reach out towards does not respond to us. Someone we have invested a lot of ourselves in turns away from us. We cannot control how people respond to us. What we have some control over is how we respond to people's response to us, how we deal with the experience of rejection. We can allow such an experience to drag us down or we can rise above it in some way.

We find an experience of rejection at the beginning of today's Gospel reading. Jesus had spent some time in Galilee proclaiming the kingdom of God in word and deed. At a certain moment, as Luke puts it, 'He resolutely took the road to Jerusalem' or in another translation, 'He set his face to go to Jerusalem'. It took a certain steeling of nerve for Jesus to head south for Jerusalem because it was a city with a reputation for killing prophets. Samaria lay between Galilee and Jerusalem. Most Jews would have gone around Samaria to get from Galilee to Jerusalem because of the hostility between Jews and Samaritans. Jesus, however, headed straight into Samaria; the Samaritans too needed to hear the good news of God's all-embracing love. He sent his disciples into a Samaritan town to prepare the way for his arrival; however, the Samaritans had no interest in welcoming a Jewish prophet who was heading for Jerusalem. Jesus was to them the outsider who could not be entertained.

There is a striking contrast between the way that Jesus responded to this experience of rejection and the way his disciples responded to it. The disciples wanted Jesus to use his influence with God to destroy this Samaritan town. This is the mindset of 'an eye for an eye', or, indeed, in this case, several eyes for one eye. I wonder what would have horrified Jesus more, the rejection of him by the Samaritans or the violent response to that rejection by his disciples? Having rebuked his disciples, Jesus' response was simply to move on to another village. He had set his face to go to Jerusalem out of love for humanity and that remained the driving force of his journey. He understood why these Samaritans responded in the way they did; he forgave them and moved on. Indeed, in the next chapter of Luke's Gospel, a little further into his journey to Jerusalem, Jesus tells the parable of the good Samaritan in which the hero is a representative of those who earlier had rejected him. There was a generosity of spirit in Jesus which was very much at odds with the attitude of his disciples; it reflected the generosity of spirit within God.

Today's Gospel reading invites us to ask ourselves, 'How do we respond to the various negative experiences that come our way in life, such as the experience of unreasonable rejection?' We can respond to such experiences in a way that doesn't do ourselves or others any good. If the disciples in the Gospel reading had gotten their way, everyone would have been diminished, including the disciples and Jesus. Taking our lead from Jesus, we can respond to such negative experiences in ways that are in keeping with what is best in us, in ways that further God's purpose for our lives and the lives of others. Jesus had the freedom to keep being his true self, his best self, even in the face of experiences that threatened to diminish him. He had the freedom to continue loving even those who rejected him, to keep seeing the good in those who gave him no reason to do so.

This is the freedom that Paul talks about in today's second reading, the freedom of the Spirit. Paul says there, 'When Christ freed us, he meant us to remain free.' What does this freedom consist of? A little later in that reading Paul spells it out, 'Serve one another in works of love.' Paul is talking about the freedom to serve others in love, regardless of how they relate to us. This, for Paul, is authentic freedom, Spirit-inspired freedom, what he calls in his letter to the Romans, 'the glorious freedom of the children of God'. Growing in this kind of freedom is one dimension of the call of Jesus to follow him, which we find in the second part of today's Gospel reading. When the disciples wanted fire from heaven to consume the Samaritans, they were not following Jesus; he had to rebuke them. Following Jesus means allowing ourselves to be led by the Spirit, so that we keep growing in the freedom of Jesus, the freedom to remain loving people, people of a generous spirit, even when the circumstances of life conspire to make us angry and bitter. If we can grow in such freedom then, in the words of the Gospel reading, we will 'spread the news of the kingdom of God' by our lives.

Fourteenth Sunday in Ordinary Time
Sharers in the Lord's work

Is 66:10–14; Gal 6:14–18; Lk 10:1–12, 17–20

Jesus often uses images from nature in his teaching. We find such an image at the beginning of today's Gospel reading. As he sends out seventy-two disciples to prepare a way for him, he says to them, 'The harvest is great but the labourers are few, so ask the Lord of the harvest to send labourers to his harvest.' Jesus could have had in mind a large grain harvest or even a large grape harvest. The soil of Galilee was fertile and good harvests were not uncommon. A lot of labourers were needed to bring in the harvest. Jesus was using imagery here. He was really referring to a different kind of harvest to the harvest that nature provides. He was suggesting that people were waiting in large numbers for the Gospel. They were waiting for labourers to bring them the Gospel. In that sense, the fields were ripe for harvest. Even though Jesus was sending out a large group of disciples, seventy-two, he, nonetheless, calls on them to ask God, the Lord of the harvest, to send out even more labourers. Seventy-two would not be enough. There was so much work to be done that many more would be needed.

Jesus' words about a great harvest and the need for many labourers are often interpreted as referencing to the need to pray for an increase in vocations to priesthood and the religious life. Though priests and religious are among the labourers that are needed in the Lord's harvest, these words have a much broader reference. The Lord needs all kinds of labourers in his harvest. We are all called to be labourers in the Lord's harvest in virtue of our Baptism. Jesus is saying that there is enormous scope to bring the Gospel of God's kingdom to people; the task is enormous and the need is great. All the followers of Jesus are needed for this work. It is not the prerogative of a select few. There has been a decline in the number of people going on for the priesthood and the religious life. It is not clear that this trend will be reversed anytime soon, at least in the Western world. In the meantime, the harvest remains great and many, many labourers are needed. The whole Church has a role to play in bringing the Gospel to others. Different people will do this in different ways, depending on their gifts and on the circumstances of their daily lives. Jesus wants to work through us all; he has a role for each one of us in his great work.

What is that work of the Lord in which we are all called to share? In the words of the Gospel reading, it is the work of proclaiming by our lives, 'The kingdom of God is very near to you ...' It is the work of making God's creative and redeeming love present in the world, so that life becomes more humane for as many people as possible. Jesus' basic message was, 'The kingdom of God is very near to you.' He gave expression to that message by bringing healing to the broken, by gathering those on the margins of society into a community where God's love could be experienced, by communicating God's forgiveness to all who felt a failure. This is what the Gospel reading refers to as 'peace', that fullness of life which God desires for all. In that sense, the term 'kingdom of God' does not only refer to what lies beyond death. It is for the here and now; it is God's just and loving will for all people now. The Gospel reading reminds us that Jesus' work of proclaiming that the kingdom of God is very near to us has been entrusted to us all, and he needs us to be faithful to this work.

It is striking in the Gospel reading that when Jesus sends out the seventy-two, he tells them that their message is to be the same, whether people welcome them or not: 'The kingdom of God is very near to you.' Their message remains good news, regardless of how that message is received. It remains the case that God and the life he offers is near to us, irrespective of people's response. The Gospel does not become bad news just because it is not welcomed. It remains what St Paul calls in his letter to the Romans, 'the power of God for salvation to everyone who has faith'. We have been entrusted with this treasure and this treasure never loses its value. It is true that, as Paul says elsewhere, we carry this treasure in clay jars, or earthen vessels. We are not worthy of the treasure that has been entrusted to us. Yet, it has been given to us and the Lord wants to work through us, frail and weak as we are. He sends us out with this treasure as labourers into his harvest, even though we may leave much to be desired. We are always being sent. The Church is the community of those who are being sent by Jesus. We are all the 'sent ones', the ones sent by Jesus with the treasure of the Gospel, just as Jesus was the one sent by God the Father with this same treasure.

Fifteenth Sunday in Ordinary Time

Indiscriminate loving

Deut 30:10-14; Col 1:15-20; Lk 10:25-37

When I went to the Holy Land with a parish group some years ago, on one of our trips we travelled down from the city of Jerusalem towards Jericho. We didn't go into Jericho but bypassed it, as we were heading for the Dead Sea. I was reminded of that journey by the parable in today's Gospel reading. That parable speaks of a man going down from Jerusalem to Jericho. It was very obvious to us on that journey that you literally go down from Jerusalem to Jericho, as Jerusalem is 2,500 feet above sea level and Jericho is over a thousand feet below sea level. Shortly after we left Jerusalem, the landscape became more and more arid. Very quickly we were into what the Gospels call the wilderness of Judea. This was not a desert in the sense in which we usually imagine the deserts of Arabia, but, rather, a hilly, rugged landscape devoid of vegetation. In Jesus' time, the road from Jerusalem to Jericho would have been no more than a basic track. Going through rugged and inhospitable terrain, it was an ideal road for robbers to launch unsuspecting attacks on unfortunate travellers. Jesus' parables were always true to life; they reflect the life-situation in which the people of that time and place lived.

The life-situation, in which we find ourselves today, two thousand years later, is very different from that of Jesus and his contemporaries, and yet the parable in our Gospel reading can speak just as powerfully to us today. The parable Jesus speaks is in answer to a question posed by an expert in the Jewish law, 'Who is my neighbour?' He wanted some help in defining who was his neighbour and who was not his neighbour. Who is the neighbour that he is expected to love? Most of Jesus' contemporaries in Israel would have understood the term 'neighbour' in the commandment to 'love your neighbour as yourself' as referring to one's fellow Israelite. They would have thought to themselves, 'Every member of the people of Israel is my neighbour. We can draw a line around the people of Israel, the descendants of the twelve tribes, and say, "These, and these alone, are my neighbours."' The story Jesus told challenged that rather narrow view of the term 'neighbour'.

When the priest and the Levite passed by the broken man on the side of the road, the listeners probably expected the next person to come along would be a Jewish lay person; however, the third person to come along, and the only one to show compassion to the broken traveller, was a Samaritan. Jews would never have considered Samaritans as their neighbours; they would never have thought that loving the neighbour included loving the Samaritans. Yet, it was the Samaritan who showed what loving the neighbour really meant. The Samaritan did not ask where this broken traveller was from or what religion he was. He was simply a needy human being, crying out for a compassionate response from another human being. When Jesus finished the parable, he asked a question of his own of the lawyer, 'Which of these three proved himself a neighbour?' It is as if Jesus was saying that 'Who is my neighbour?' is the wrong question. What matters is to be a neighbour, and those who are good neighbours to others don't ask the question, 'Who is my neighbour?' The Samaritan was not preoccupied with the question, 'Who is my neighbour?' When he came upon the broken traveller, he did not ask, 'Is this the neighbour I should love or not?' It is likely that a man left half dead on the road from Jerusalem to Jericho would have been a Jew. This likelihood was neither here nor there in the eyes of the Samaritan; here was a human being in desperate need and that is all that mattered.

The expert in the Jewish law was concerned to make distinctions. Who is my neighbour and who is not? Who am I obliged to love and who am I not obliged to love? The Samaritan in the story made no such distinctions. To that extent, he was very much a Jesus figure. Jesus did not make distinctions either. He shared table with all sorts; he offered God's hospitality to all of humanity, without distinction. His love, his mission, was indiscriminate. In the words of the second reading, it embraced 'everything in heaven and everything on earth'. In telling the parable of the good Samaritan, Jesus put himself into the story in and through the figure of the Samaritan, the outsider, the other. Just as the Samaritan is a Jesus figure, we are all called to be Jesus figures. In the words of Jesus at the end of the Gospel reading, we are all called to 'go and do the same' ourselves. Clearly, we have a special love for our family and our closest friends; there are emotional bonds there which cannot easily be replicated. Yet, beyond those bonds of natural affection, Jesus is calling us to be indiscriminate in the way we relate to others, especially to those in great need. The parable seems to be saying that the common humanity that unites us is a much more significant reality than the differences of nationality, race or religion that may distinguish us. If that simple but profound message was taken to heart by all, there would surely be less people left for dead by the roadsides of life.

Sixteenth Sunday in Ordinary Time
The hospitality of presence

Gn 18:1-10; Col 1:24-8; Lk 10:38-42

Many of us have aunts that were almost like a second mother to us when we were growing up. I was fortunate to have two such aunts. They were my mother's older sisters. Neither of them ever married. They lived together in my maternal grandparents' house until they needed to live in a more supportive environment. One of my aunts was ninety when she died and the other was ninety-six. When myself and my brothers were children, they came to our house every Thursday night to let my parents off for the night to the cinema. They were very different in temperament and, yet, they were inseparable. One of them, Addie, always reminded me of Martha. She was always doing something for others, whether it was cleaning the house, or cooking a meal, or washing clothes or one hundred and one other things. My other aunt, Eve, reminded me of Mary, Martha's sister. You wouldn't find her down on her knees scrubbing a floor like Addie. She tended to sit quietly, often reading. Yet, she was a great listener and there was a very lovely quality to her quiet presence. Myself and my siblings loved our two aunts deeply. We loved each of them in different ways. They were both equally hospitable people, but they expressed their hospitable nature in very different ways. We were all equally graced by the hospitable spirit of these wonderful women.

Hospitality is a very important value in the Gospels. Jesus himself was very hospitable to people. Indeed, he came to reveal the hospitality of God, especially to those who were most in need of it. Of all the four Gospels, it is the Gospel of Luke, from which we are reading this liturgical year, that highlights Jesus as the revelation of God's hospitality. Perhaps this is why in this Gospel, more than any other, Jesus seems to spend so much time at people's tables, especially at the table of those considered beyond the scope of God's embrace, 'tax collectors and sinners'. In Luke's Gospel, Jesus is also portrayed as accepting hospitality from others. In a story that is unique to this Gospel, two disciples invite the risen Lord to be a guest at their table in Emmaus. In today's Gospel reading Jesus is offered hospitality by two sisters. Martha seems to be the more senior of the two, and Mary the more marginal. It is said of Martha that she welcomed Jesus to her house. Martha's way of showing hospitality was to roll up her sleeves and prepare an elaborate meal, apparently in a rather anxious frame of mind. Her anxious activity seems to have left her rather angry with her sister, Mary, who she felt was not carrying her weight sufficiently. She comes across as angry with Jesus too for not giving Mary a telling off, 'Lord, do you not care that my sister is leaving me to do the serving all by myself? Please, tell her to help me.' I think many of us find it easy to identify with Martha. We can all feel a bit put upon from time to time. We sense that if only so-and-so would pull his or her weight, our life would be a lot easier. We can all get into an overly anxious frame of mind about all we have to do, and our anxious, self-pitying, spirit can quench the Holy Spirit in us somewhat. It is Paul in one of his letters who reminds us that 'God loves a cheerful giver'.

Mary was showing Jesus a different kind of hospitality to Martha. She was sitting at his feet, listening to what Jesus had to say. It was traditional for students to sit at the feet of the rabbi when the rabbi was teaching. Mary was taking up the posture of a disciple, a pupil of Jesus. She wanted to hear what he had to say; she was trying to drink in his word. In the Gospels we often find Jesus defending people against the criticism of others. On this occasion he defends Mary against Martha's criticism, but does so in a way that is very respectful of, and even affectionate towards, Martha. It is very rare in the Gospels that Jesus addresses someone by their personal name twice, as here, 'Martha, Martha'. Jesus clearly loved both sisters very much; yet, he wanted to validate the kind of hospitality that Mary was showing him, the hospitality of attentive listening, the hospitality of presence. On this occasion it seems that this was the kind of hospitality that Jesus actually desired – 'Mary has chosen the better part' – rather than the anxious-filled hospitality of Martha's activity.

This passage follows immediately after Jesus speaks the parable of the good Samaritan. This parable shows that there is a time for anxious activity in the service of others, especially the most vulnerable; yet, there is also a time for being present to someone who has something important to say to us. We always need to ask, 'What is it that love requires of me at this moment, under these circumstances? How can I best serve this person?' In terms of our relationship with Jesus, there is a time to actively serve him, as one of his labourers, and there is a time to listen in silence to his word. Both are important in their time. The spirits of Mary and Martha are both needed at different times.

Seventeenth Sunday in Ordinary Time
Jesus' teaching on prayer

Gn 18:20-32; Col 2:12-14; Lk 11:1-13

When it comes to prayer, we can all feel a little inadequate. We often sense that our prayer is not all it could be. The sense that we are not praying well can often leave us discouraged. Saint Paul was aware of how we can struggle to pray. That is why in his letter to the Romans he says, 'We do not know how to pray as we ought.' He then immediately declares, 'The Spirit helps us in our weakness ... that very Spirit intercedes with sighs too deep for words.' Paul is saying that a wordless prayer of the Spirit is going on deep within us, even as we struggle to pray. One of the roles of the Spirit in our lives is to help us to pray. The Spirit's help in the area of prayer is a continuation of Jesus' help. In today's Gospel reading, Jesus teaches his disciples how to pray, in response to their request, 'Lord, teach us to pray'.

The Gospels portray Jesus at prayer many times, and sometimes they give us the content of his prayer; however, only once is Jesus presented as teaching his disciples a prayer for them to pray, the prayer that has become known as the Lord's Prayer. The prayer that Jesus gives us has few words. It is a prayer that is paired down to its essentials. It is short but deep. In giving us this prayer, Jesus was also giving us a lesson on how to pray. It is a school of prayer. For Jesus the primary focus of his life was God his father, which is why the opening petitions all relate to God, the honouring or hallowing of God's name, and the coming of God's kingdom. They are really variations of one petition. When God's kingdom comes to earth, God's name will be held holy. At the beginning of this prayer, Jesus is teaching us to look beyond ourselves to God's purpose, yielding to what is due to God alone.

Only after those petitions that focus on God does Jesus teach us to focus on our own needs in a second set of petitions. We are to prayer for our daily bread, all that we need each day for our journey through the present world. It is an imperfect world. We ourselves are imperfect and we have to deal with imperfect people and, so, we will always stand in need of God's forgiveness and we will always need the freedom to allow the forgiveness we receive from God to flow through us and embrace those who offend us. In this world, we will be assailed by evil in various forms, which will often put our faith to the test. We need to ask God to keep us faithful when the test comes, so that we don't succumb to evil but, rather, as Paul says, overcome evil with good. It is significant that in those second set of petitions, Jesus teaches us to focus not on ourselves as individuals but as members of a community. The language of the second part of the prayer is 'us' and 'our' rather than 'me' and 'my'. In praying those petitions, I am praying not just for myself but for others. Through the two sets of petitions that make up the Lord's Prayer, Jesus is teaching us that prayer is always a going out of ourselves towards God and towards others.

After this teaching on prayer, Jesus, in the Gospel reading, develops his teaching with two images, one drawn from village life in Galilee and the other from family life within the village. A villager who finds he has nothing to offer an unexpected guest should be able to rely on a friend within the village to help him out in his need, even at midnight. A son who asks his father for food, whether it is bread, fish or an egg, can expect to be given what he asks for. In between these two little scenarios, Jesus gives an instruction based on both images, 'Ask, and it will be given to you …'. If someone in a small village can rely on a good friend to help him out in an emergency and if a son can rely on his father to feed him, how much more can we rely on God in our need? Because God is our heavenly father, we can confidently ask him for our fundamental needs; we can search after God in the expectation of finding; we can knock on God's door in the expectation of having it opened. What are we to ask God for, above all else? Jesus has already shown what we need to ask for in the petitions of the Lord's Prayer. At the very end of the Gospel reading, Jesus suggests that what we also need to ask for is the Holy Spirit, 'How much more will the heavenly father give the Holy Spirit to those who ask him?' Even if our prayer of petition is not answered in the way we would like, such prayer will always open us up to God's gift of the Holy Spirit. Pentecost is a daily event for those who persevere with the prayer of petition, who keep coming before God in their need, with hearts open to God's gift. In this way, our persevering prayer is never wasted; it changes us, enabling us to grow into God's will for our lives.

Eighteenth Sunday in Ordinary Time
Who am I becoming?

Qo 1:2, 2:21–3; Col 3:1–5, 9–11; Lk 12:13–21

I recently came across a Jewish story from the tradition of the Jewish rabbis. Rabbinic Judaism, as it is often called, began in earnest just after the period of the New Testament and has continued to this day. This is how the story goes. A man had two sons, one rich and one poor. The rich son had no children. His poorer brother was blessed with many sons and daughters. On the death of their father, they each received half of his land as their inheritance. The rich son began to worry, saying to himself, 'I am rich, with bread enough and to spare, while my brother and his family are poor, with scarcely enough to eat, although they trust in God's providence. I will move the landmark that indicates the boundary of our two properties so that my brother will have more land than me, and so the prospect of more crops to harvest.' The poor brother too was worried and could not sleep, saying to himself, 'Here I am, surrounded by the riches of a wife and children, while my brother daily faces the shame and sorrow of having no children. He deserves to have more of our inherited land to compensate him for his great poverty.' The next night the two brothers arose, and each went to move the landmark. There they met, embracing one another with tears. And there on that spot was built the holy temple of Jerusalem. Still today, wherever sisters and brothers love and share, there is holy ground; there God is worshipped and praised.

This is an inheritance story where the two sons who inherit their father's estate are both exemplary characters. They each held their inheritance lightly and each was moved to share some of it with his sibling who he perceived to be in greater need. We probably know from our experience that not all inheritance stories reveal the more generous side of human nature. Indeed, inheritances can sometimes cause tensions and disputes within families. In today's Gospel reading, a man approaches Jesus and asks him to intervene in an inheritance dispute within his family. He wants Jesus to take his side against his brother. Jesus refuses to take on the role of arbitrator that he is being offered. Instead, he seizes the opportunity to warn against the vice of greed. Rather than go on at length about this, he does what seems to have come natural to him. He tells a story. The story Jesus tells is unusual in having only one human character in it. There is no room in this story for anyone else because there is no room in this man's life for anyone else. When the rich man speaks, he speaks to himself and his speech to himself is full of the little words 'I' and 'my'. He speaks of 'my crops', 'my barns', 'my grain' and 'my soul'. It is a portrait of someone completely absorbed by his possessions. He looked to secure his life by focusing on his possessions, his crops and on his achievements, building bigger barns. Just when he seems to have his security nailed down, another character enters the story, not a human character but God. God's assessment of this man's underlying attitude is stark, 'Fool!' The message of the story is that this man's approach to life is the height of folly. This kind of self-absorption does not bring the security that was sought after; it carries no weight at the hour of death. It leaves one poor in the eyes of God. It has been said that when we go to meet the Lord, we leave behind everything we have acquired and achieved and we take with us everything we are and have become. The question that matters at the end of our lives is not 'What do I possess?' or 'What have I achieved?' but 'Who have I become?'

A question we all need to live with as we go through life is, 'Who am I becoming?' In today's second reading Paul points us in the direction of an answer to that question. He speaks of putting on a new self, and he equates that with a self that is renewed in the image of its creator. We are to become more and more an image of God, the Creator. God's creativity always moves out to others. God creates for others. We too are to live creatively, living for others, thereby reflecting the character of God. The perfect image of God the Creator is Jesus. He lived for others. He emptied himself, making himself poor, so that others could be enriched. He died so that others could live. He thereby reveals the character of God the Creator and reveals the person we are all called to become. Whenever, like Jesus, we are creative for others, whenever, like him, our presence is life-giving for others, then we are being renewed in the image of God the Creator and we are becoming rich in the sight of God. The parable Jesus speaks suggests that the real issue concerns where the focus is in our lives. Is it on myself or on God and those God loves? In that sense, the problem is not the possessions themselves but how tightly we cling to them and how creatively we make use of them for others.

Nineteenth Sunday in Ordinary Time

Following the Lord's way

Wis 18:6-9; Heb 11:1-2, 8-19; Lk 12:32-48

This is the time of the year when traditionally people go on holidays. When we think of holidays we usually think in terms of setting out on some kind of a journey, whether it is a long journey or a relatively short one. While we are on the journey we tend to keep looking ahead. We keep our destination in mind. To be on a journey is to be on our way towards somewhere and our destination is always present to us even while we are still on our way. It shapes our journey and influences how we journey.

The Christian life has often been understood as a journey. At the very beginning of his ministry Jesus called on people to follow him, to set out on a journey behind him. Jesus' own ministry was a series of journeys, initially in Galilee, and then a last fateful journey to Jerusalem. In the course of his ministry he not only called on his disciples to follow him but he also sent them on missionary journeys. When he appeared to his disciples after rising from the dead, he again called on them to go and to make disciples of all nations. They were to set out on a journey that involved walking in the way of Jesus and calling on others to walk that same way. According to the Acts of the Apostles, the first disciples were called followers of the Way. As disciples of the Lord, we are following a way. We are trying to follow the Lord's way; we seek to take him as our Way. The image of the way for our Christian life suggests that there is nothing static about our faith. Faith is a dynamic reality. It is about always being on the way, always standing ready to go where the Lord is calling us, always leaving ourselves open to where the Spirit is leading us. The Lord is always calling us; the Spirit is always leading us. We are always trying to heed that call and follow that lead.

Every journey has a destination; it is a journey towards somewhere. As followers of the Lord, we too have a destination. The second reading today speaks of that destination as a 'city founded, designed and built by God'. This is our ultimate destination, what the New Testament elsewhere calls the heavenly city, the new and eternal Jerusalem. That second reading was a reflection on the journey of Abraham and Sarah. According to the author of the letter to the Hebrews, on all of their earthly journeys, they always had this heavenly destination in mind. They were constantly looking beyond all earthly destinations. Even when they reached the long-awaited Promised Land, they did not fully settle there, because they knew it was not their final destination. God's promises were not completely fulfilled by the gift of the Promised Land, great as that blessing was. As the reading declares, they saw what God had promised as in the far distance, recognising that they were only strangers and nomads on this earth. They realised that their true homeland lay beyond this world. Even when they reached the Promised Land, they continued to journey on in hope. This is how we journey too. As Paul says in his letter to the Philippians, 'Our homeland is in heaven, and it is from there that we are expecting a Saviour.' That is why within the Christian tradition the Christian life is often spoken of as a pilgrimage. A pilgrimage is a journey of faith towards a place of encounter with God. Every earthly pilgrimage, be it a pilgrimage to Knock or Lourdes or Rome or Santiago de Compostela or Jerusalem, is the Christian journey in miniature.

Because we are on a journey towards a destination, as on all journeys, we keep our destination in view. We recognise that, in the language of the Gospel reading today, our 'treasure' is not to be found in this world. Our treasure is beyond this world. In the words of Jesus in our Gospel reading, it is 'in heaven where no thief can reach it and no moth destroy it'. Because this is our treasure, it is where our heart is too. We keep our ultimate destination in our heart as we journey.

Like Abraham and Sarah, we look forward to a city founded, designed and built by God. Our journey of faith is at the same time a journey of hope. We hope for realities that at present remain unseen. This way of journeying does not remove us from this earthly life in any way. Rather, when we arrive at our destination we want the Lord to see us, in the language of the Gospel reading, 'Dressed for action with our lamps lit.' We want to meet the Lord with the light of our faith burning brightly, a light that has shown itself in good works, in works of love on behalf of others. As Jesus says on one occasion, 'Let your light shine before others, so that they may see your good works and give glory to your father in heaven.' This is a call to be awake to reality here and now, to allow the light of our faith to shine brightly, as we continue our hopeful journey towards the future that God has prepared for us.

Twentieth Sunday in Ordinary Time
Running steadily in the race

Jer 38:4–6, 8–10; Heb 12:1–4; Lk 12:49–53

There is something very exciting about well-trained athletes racing together, each one striving to be the first over the line. Many people enjoy watching runners competing against each other in various tract events, whether it be the 100-yard dash or the longer track events.

In the ancient world, especially in the Greek world, games involving highly trained athletes were hugely popular. The Olympic Games were the most famous of these games. Other famous games were the Isthmian Games that took place close to the city of Corinth. Such games were part of the cultural environment of those who wrote the various books that we find in the New Testament. It is not surprising that they sometimes make use of the imagery of these games for their own purposes. We find a very good example of this in today's second reading. The author of the letter to the Hebrews imagines the Christian life as a race. In the races that were a feature of the various games, athletes freed themselves of anything that might have a negative impact on their speed. In a similar way, the second reading calls on us to throw off everything that might hinder us, that might hold us back from running the race that the Lord is calling us to run. The author identifies the greatest hindrance as 'the sin that clings so easily'. We all have something we need to throw off because it is holding us back from running well the race that we began on the day of our Baptism. This 'throwing off' is not something we do once and that is it. Every day we need to pray, 'Lord, be merciful to me a sinner; Lord, help me to throw off whatever is holding me back from becoming the person you are calling me to be.'

The second reading develops this imagery of the Christian life as a race in another way. When athletes compete in a race, they are always focused. They keep their focus on the finishing line. As we try to run the race of the Christian life, we too need a clear focus. In the words of that second reading, 'Let us not lose sight of Jesus, who leads us in our faith, and brings it to perfection.' The focus of our lives is not to be our failings but the Lord. If we keep him in view, everything else, including our failings, will find its proper level. As our reading states, we keep the Lord in view as someone who is leading us in our faith and bringing it to perfection. The Lord is out ahead of us; we are following his lead. He is also residing deep within us, working to deepen and strengthen our faith.

That second reading develops this imagery of the life of faith as a race in yet another way. A good athlete will do his or her best to stay in the race, to keep striving for the finish line. In a similar way, the second reading calls on us to 'keep running steadily in the race that we have started'. The author was aware that the people he was writing to were suffering because of their faith in the Lord. Like Jesus, they encountered opposition. They may have been tempted to give up the race, to lose faith. Jesus makes reference to such opposition in the Gospel reading, suggesting that it can come even from within the families of his disciples. We can all struggle with that temptation to lose faith, especially when our faith is put to the test in various ways, as it often is today. At such times, we need to keep running steadily in the race we have started. It is by keeping our focus on the Lord that we will be enabled to keep running when the temptation to give up or to turn aside is strong. It is the Lord who empowers us to stay in the race. It is his Spirit, the Holy Spirit, who keeps us going. Jesus makes reference to the Holy Spirit in today's Gospel reading. He declares, 'I have come to bring fire to the earth, and how I wish it were blazing already!' He is referring there to the enlivening and purifying fire of the Spirit. The Holy Spirit is our great resource in this race we have started and one of the great prayers of the Christian tradition is,

'Come, Holy Spirit, fill my heart and enkindle in me the fire of your love.' The second reading reminds us that in this race we have another source of support, what it calls the 'great cloud' of witnesses on every side of us. These are the people in whom the Spirit is alive and who inspire us by their living of their faith. Many of them are living among us, on every side of us. Others are with the Lord in heaven. All are our companions in the race.

Not every element of a race can be applied to the Christian life. In a competitive race, there can only be one winner. The Christian life is not a competition. We are moving together towards the one goal and we are called to support each other as we try to keep running steadily in the race that is before us.

Twenty-First Sunday in Ordinary Time
Will only a few be saved?

Is 66:18–21; Heb 12:5–7, 11–13; Lk 13:22–30

A questioning spirit is in no way alien to a life of faith. Indeed, faith will always generate questions, especially the kind of question to which there is no definitive answer. Saint Paul in one of his letters declares, 'Now we see, as in a mirror, dimly.' The seeing of faith is always a partial seeing. We do not yet 'see face to face', in the words of Paul. To believe is to learn to live with very big questions that cannot be fully answered in this life. Faith is always seeking to understand what is believed. It is a journey of discovery. In the Gospels, people of faith address all kinds of questions to Jesus. We have an example of such questioning at the beginning of today's Gospel reading. Someone comes up to Jesus and asks him, 'Sir, will there be only a few saved?' Jesus has been proclaiming the presence of the kingdom of God. This man was wondering if only a select few would enter this kingdom. Is the kingdom of God for the few or for the many?

When Jesus is asked a question in the Gospels, he doesn't always answer it directly. Rather than just giving the information that is asked for, his answer often invites people to reflect on what he is saying. Jesus' response to this man's question has many elements to it. Towards the end of his response, towards the end of our Gospel reading, there is a statement of Jesus which does respond directly to the man's question. Jesus declares that people 'from east and west, from north and south, will come to take their places at the feast in the kingdom of God'. 'Will only a few be saved?' Jesus seems to answer 'no'. On the contrary, there will be people from the four corners of the earth present at the banquet of eternal life. The great Jewish patriarchs, Abraham, Isaac and Jacob, won't just have Jewish people for company at that banquet; they will have all sorts with them. Indeed, there is no telling who is coming to dinner in the kingdom of God. This message of Jesus is in keeping with the vision of the prophet Isaiah in the first reading. There Isaiah announces that the Lord will gather the nations of every language in Jerusalem. Isaiah even goes so far as to say that the Lord will make some members of these pagan peoples priests and Levites. Jesus identifies with this very inclusive vision of Isaiah in today's Gospel reading from Luke. In the Gospel of John, Jesus speaks of heaven as his father's house in which there are many rooms. This image of heaven as a many-roomed house suggests again that there is room for all sorts. At the very end of today's Gospel reading, Jesus declares that 'those now last will be first'. Those whom many people in his time would have considered unsuited to the kingdom of God may well have a place of honour. Jesus' response to the question, 'Will there be only a few saved?' suggests that God's embrace is much wider than we could conceive. Saint Paul expresses this truth in his own way when he speaks of 'the breadth and length and height and depth' of the love of God revealed in Jesus.

There is another dimension to Jesus' response. He deflects the person's question about numbers and, instead, he issues a personal challenge to him, 'Try your best to enter by the narrow door', or the narrow gate. In the Gospel of John, Jesus identifies himself as the door or the gate. He is calling on us to enter the kingdom of God through him. There was nothing narrow about Jesus. His vision would have been experienced as disturbingly broad and inclusive by many. In speaking of the door or the gate as narrow, he is suggesting that a certain focus of mind and heart is called for. We can't just saunter through a narrow gate without watching where we are going. We have to be careful and deliberate about it. In saying 'try your best' to enter by the narrow door, Jesus is suggesting that an element of self-discipline is called for so as to focus on what is required. The clarity of focus that is required to go through a narrow gate finds expression in one of Jesus' beatitudes, 'Blessed are the pure in heart, for they shall see God.' A certain purity or clarity of intention is required and this is revealed in the choices that we make on a daily basis. We can never underestimate God's desire and determination to gather people of all sorts to his table of life, but Jesus is reminding us that we each have a part to play. There is a gate we need to go through, if God's desire for our lives is to come to pass. The gate is always open. Jesus is always an open door. No one can close it. Yet, we have to keep passing through it. Every day we need to choose to follow Jesus, to keep learning to live like him, to keep inviting the Holy Spirit to fill us with Jesus' love for God and humanity.

Twenty-Second Sunday in Ordinary Time
Humbling ourselves before God

Sir 3:17–20, 28–9; Heb 12:18–19, 22–4; Lk 14:1, 7–14

More often than not, when you go to a wedding reception you find that the tables all have the names of guests on them. You go to a board and see where you have been seated and then take your place at the table. When someone has already decided where you are to sit, it takes the pressure off having to decide for yourself. I am sure that deciding who sits where and with whom must be a challenging task for the couple or their families.

In today's Gospel reading, Jesus is the guest at a meal hosted by a leading Pharisee. The reading says that he was invited because the host and his fellow Pharisees wanted to take a close look at him; they wanted to suss him out. At table, Jesus speaks a parable to them. On the surface the parable is about the seating arrangements at wedding feasts. The parable presupposes the situation where guests are not assigned a seat but choose their own seat. Some people who think more of themselves than they should find a place of honour as near as possible to the married couple, what we used to call, 'the top table'. The parable suggests that this is a risky strategy because they may be asked to go further down the line. Alternatively, those who are low-key about themselves and who take a correspondingly low-key seat may find themselves being invited to take what would be considered a more honourable place. In the parable Jesus is depicting a scene that would have been very recognisable at the time. People could imagine it happening.

All of Jesus' parables are stories about day-to-day life in his culture and time, but at another level they say something about our relationship with God. That is hinted at in the very short comment Jesus makes following on from the parable, 'Everyone who exalts himself, will be humbled [by God], and everyone who humbles himself will be exalted [by God]'. The parable, then, is calling on us to humble ourselves before God, rather than exalt ourselves before God. It is probably true to say that 'humility' is a virtue that is not really in vogue today. Maybe that is because humility can easily be confused with attitudes that are not humble at all. Humility is certainly not putting ourselves down or denying or making little of our gifts and abilities. It is not about pretending that we do not have some gift when, in fact, we do. Real humility is about truth, the truth about ourselves, and the truth about our relationship with God. Humility is first of all clarity and honesty about ourselves, the gifts and talents we have, and the gifts we don't have, our limitations. Humility is also about the truth of our relationship with God. We recognise that the gifts, the abilities, the strengths we have are ultimately gifts from God. They do not make us boastful but grateful and responsible, recognising that those gifts have been given to us for the service of others. Those who exalt themselves, in the language of today's Gospel reading, are those who are so full of their own abilities and virtues that they lose sight of their ultimate dependence on God. Humility calls on us to recognise who we truly are, namely, God's creatures who have been greatly blessed and gifted by God and who are completely dependent on him for everything.

It has often been pointed out that the word 'humility' is derived from the Latin word 'humus', which means earth. So when we are advised to humble ourselves, it is an invitation to be grounded, to be attentive to our connectedness with the earth, and with everyone on it, and with God the Creator of all. Humble people recognise that everyone, regardless of their circumstances, and, indeed, the whole created world, shares in an interconnection of life given by God. It was above all Jesus who was humble in that sense of being earthed and grounded and connected to all who are on this earth and of this earth. He tried to connect with all sorts of people and he invited them to connect with him. In today's Gospel reading we find him sharing table with wealthy Pharisees. He also shared table with the kind of people that the Pharisees would run a mile from, tax collectors and sinners, the poor and the disabled. At the end of the Gospel reading, Jesus goes on to call on his Pharisee host to invite to this table not just his own rich neighbours and friends, his own kind, but the poor, the crippled, the lame and the blind.

The humble person recognises the truth of our interconnectedness under God and our communal dependence on God, and then relates to others and to the earth out of that awareness. In spite of our many differences, we all have a common humanity, we are all children of the one God, we are all made in God's image, and we are all equally loved and esteemed by God. Indeed, according to the second reading, our ultimate destiny, beyond this earthly life, is to belong to a universal community in which everyone is a firstborn and a citizen of heaven.

Twenty-Third Sunday in Ordinary Time
Understanding the Lord's way

Wis 9:13-18; Phm 9-10, 12-17; Lk 14:25-33

Coming to know one person well is the journey of a lifetime. Even when we think we know someone well, something can happen to make us realise that we don't know the person as well as we thought. There is a profound mystery to each person. Faithful love can help to plumb some of the depths of those we love, and, yet, there remains a core that we can never fully grasp. The author of today's first reading from the Book of Wisdom declares that it is hard for us 'to work out what is on earth, laborious to know what is within our reach'. We labour to really know what is within our reach, whether that is the universe as a whole or the one closest to us in love. The conclusion drawn by this author from this truth is 'Who can know the intentions of God?' 'Who can divine the will of the Lord?'

If we struggle to understand what is within our reach, how much more will we struggle to know God? Saint Paul wrote a powerful letter to the Church of Rome. It is above all in this letter that we find Paul seeking to communicate to others his understanding of his faith in God. After eleven dense chapters, he declares, 'O the depths of the riches and wisdom and knowledge of God! How unsearchable are his judgements and how inscrutable his ways!' He had immersed himself in seeking to understand the mystery of God's way of relating to us through his son, Jesus, and the Holy Spirit, but he had to accept that there was more to God than he could ever understand in this life. He was convinced that in the next life, when we see God face to face, the veil will finally be lifted. As he says in his first letter to the Corinthians, 'Then I will know fully, even as I have been fully known.'

It is not surprising then that we sometimes struggle to understand the person of Jesus and to make sense of some of the things he says.

We might find ourselves struggling to make sense of Jesus' opening statement in today's Gospel reading, 'If anyone comes to me without hating his father, mother, wife, children, brothers, sisters, yes and his own life too, he cannot be my disciple.' Elsewhere Jesus calls on us to love our neighbour as ourselves and he understands the term 'neighbour' to include even our enemy. How then can he call on us to hate the members of our family? At a surface level, Jesus seems to be very inconsistent and, even, unreasonable. What are we to make of this saying? Jesus was a Jew and he often used a Semitic idiom that can seem strange to our ears. The language of loving/hating was a Semitic way of expressing preference. If you prefer one thing or one person over another, you are said to 'love' the one and 'hate' the other. Jesus is saying to his disciples that he is to be preferred even over those with whom we have the strongest ties of affection. He is calling for a love that was normally reserved for God. It is God who is to be loved with all one's heart, soul, strength and mind. Jesus, as God's representative, God's son, is asking for that same quality of love that is due to God alone. The giving of our heart, soul, strength and mind to Jesus in love does not remove us from those for whom we have a natural affection. Rather, it enables us to love them in the selfless way the Lord loves them, to love them for themselves rather than for ourselves, to love them in a manner that promotes their ultimate good, rather than in any self-serving way. The Gospels as a whole suggest that if our relationship with the Lord is the primary relationship in our life, then all our human relationships are more likely to have the loving quality that God desires and intends for them. If we can imbibe the Lord's values and attitudes, his mind and heart, then the Lord will love others through us and our love will be truly life-giving for others.

This is what Paul asks of Philemon in today's second reading. Philemon, a convert of Paul, was the leader of a house church. His slave, Onesimus, ran away and made his way to Paul, who was in prison. It seems that Paul brought Onesimus to faith in Jesus. That is why Paul refers to him as a 'child of mine', a spiritual son. Paul sends Onesimus back to Philemon and calls on Philemon to receive him no longer as a slave but as a brother in the Lord. Paul is saying to Philemon, 'If your relationship with the Lord is the primary relationship in your life, you must relate to your slave no longer as a slave but as a brother.' If Philemon does what Paul asks of him, then the Lord's vision for human living begins to come to pass. When our relationship with the Lord is the primary relationship in our life, all our human relationships are enhanced. They become more fully human in the way God intended.

Twenty-Fourth Sunday in Ordinary Time
The extravagant ways of God

Ex 32:7-11, 13-14; 1 Tm 1:12-17; Lk 15:1-32

Recently somebody asked me a question about the behaviour of the shepherd in the first of the three parables in today's Gospel reading. Why would a shepherd leave ninety-nine sheep in the wilderness and go after the missing one until he had found it? Surely, in doing so, the shepherd ran the risk of all ninety-nine rambling off and getting lost. People who first heard that parable would probably think that the shepherd was a bit obsessive about the lost sheep and that his behaviour was somewhat extravagant. Not only was it foolish to leave ninety-nine sheep on their own but putting the lost sheep on his shoulders seems a bit much too. Shepherds would not usually behave in the way the shepherd behaves in this story.

It is not so much the story of an average shepherd but the story of an exceptional shepherd, and the exceptional shepherd in the story that Jesus told was intended as an image of God, and also an image of Jesus himself who reveals God. It is as if Jesus is saying, 'God's ways are not our ways'. God's way of relating to God's people is not typical of how most shepherds relate to their flocks. Jesus seems to be saying that God has a passion for those who are lost in any way, those who find themselves separated, isolated and alone. Although some people may seem to be more obviously lost than others, in reality, we are all lost in some part of ourselves. In one way or another, we have all wandered away, from the Lord, from the Church, from the way of life the Lord is calling us to live. Jesus is saying in the parable of the shepherd that God is seeking us out in that place where we are most lost, where we are most alienated from God, from others and from ourselves.

In the third parable, the figure of the father is as unrealistic a figure as the shepherd. Just as most shepherds would not abandon ninety-nine sheep in the wilderness to go in search of one lost sheep, so most fathers would not throw a feast for a son who had behaved so shamefully. By demanding his share of the inheritance before it was due to him on the death of his father, the younger son was saying to his father, 'As far as I am concerned, you are as good as dead.' Having taken what didn't really belong to him, he then wastes it on a life of self-indulgence, and it is only because he found himself near to death that he started to head back home as a last-ditch survival strategy. No human father in that culture would have run to such a son while the son was still a long way off, showered him with hugs and kisses, dressed him up to the nines, and then killed the most prized animal on the farm for a celebratory homecoming feast. When the people of Jesus' day first heard that story, they would certainly have asked, 'What sort of a fool is this father?' 'Has he no self-respect?' Yet, once again Jesus was saying, 'God's ways are not our ways.' The father in this story is an even more striking figure than the shepherd in the first story. When sheep ramble off and get lost, the category of blame does not really apply to them; that's what sheep do, they ramble. However, when a grown son rambles off in the way the son in the parable does, there is plenty of reason to apportion blame. Thoughtless, selfish, self-centred, insensitive, arrogant, headstrong – all those qualities, and more, apply to the younger son. Yet the father treats him with even greater affection than the shepherd treats the lost sheep.

What the shepherd and the father have in common is that they both brought the lost home. Jesus is saying, this is what God is about and this is what I am about. He also seems to be saying that 'repentance', coming home, is much more about allowing ourselves to be found by a searching God than it is about anything we ourselves do. Yes, we have a role to play – the son staggered in the direction of home – however, our role is tiny in comparison to God's role. Our coming home to God, to each other, to ourselves, is the work of God above all; it is the work of grace. Our role consists of allowing God's grace to work in us. Saint Paul was very aware of this from his own experience. In the second reading, he declares that he was the greatest of sinners because of all he did to injure and discredit the faith. Yet, he goes on to say, 'The grace of our Lord filled me with faith and with the love that is in Christ Jesus.'

The elder son in the parable was horrified at his father's behaviour; he appears to have been as angry at his father as he was at his younger brother. He was like the Pharisees and the scribes who were scandalised by the way Jesus welcomed sinners and ate with them. The elder son represents all those who are scandalised by the God revealed in Jesus, who sit in judgement of a God whose searching love stops at nothing to bring the lost home again. God's searching love embraces those who are lost in this way too, calling on them to come in from the cold and rejoice in God's way of relating to us.

Twenty-Fifth Sunday in Ordinary Time
Crisis as opportunity

Am 8:4-7; 1 Tm 2:1-8; Lk 16:1-13

Most of us hit a crisis at one time or another in our lives. A relationship with someone may bring a lot of struggle and pain. Our health or the health of someone we love may take a turn for the worst. We may suddenly experience a significant loss, whether the loss of a job, or the loss of our independence or the loss of a loved one. Such times of crisis bring home to us what it is that really matters and what is not so important. We can come to value in a new way what we were inclined to take for granted, and come to take less seriously what we once gave a lot of time and attention. Invariably, a personal crisis of one kind or another teaches us that what really matters to us is the people in our lives. A crisis often brings home to us our dependence on others, how much we need them, how much they matter to us. The things in our life become less important; the people in our life become more important to us.

In the parable that Jesus speaks in today's Gospel reading, a steward suddenly finds himself in a crisis situation when his employer, the rich owner of the estate, calls him up and gives him his notice because he had been wasteful with his employer's property. Perhaps he was guilty of the ancient equivalent of putting his hand into the till. In the crisis situation in which he suddenly found himself, he took decisive action with a view to gaining friends, building up a bank of goodwill so that when the day came that he had to leave his job there would be people out there who would welcome him into their homes. Whatever might be thought about the morality of what he did in significantly reducing people's debts to his master, his crisis brought home to him the importance of people in his life. He knew that when the storm broke, he would need other people around him, and, rather late in the day, he set about ensuring that such people would be there when he needed them. The steward in this parable is not much of a hero, just as the younger son in last Sunday's parable wasn't much of a hero either. Yet, Jesus was prepared to tell stories about very flawed people who, nonetheless, had something to teach us. In the parable of today's Gospel reading, even the steward's employer has to grudgingly acknowledge the steward's astuteness. Just as the steward's world was about to collapse, he finally got his priorities right. He used money, while he still had control of it, to win him friends, recognising that friends are a more valuable commodity than money, and that people are a much greater treasure than all the material possessions in the world.

One of the morals Jesus draws from the parable that he tells is, 'Use money, tainted as it is, to win your friends, and thus make sure that when it fails you, they will welcome you into the tents of eternity.' We all gather an enormous amount of stuff as we go through life; anyone who has had to move house knows that only too well. Sooner or later, we have to let it all go; we can't take it with us as we leave this life. In that sense, in the words of Jesus in the Gospel reading, our material possessions fail us, they do not endure; however, the relationships that we form in life do endure. Saint Paul in his great hymn to love in his first letter to the Corinthians says that love never ends. Authentic love endures beyond the grave into eternity. Jesus speaks about the friends we make in this life welcoming us into the tents of eternity. When there was more money around than there is today, people spoke a lot about the importance of investments. Those with money to spare often wonder how best to invest it so as to get the greatest return on it. The Gospel reading today, and, indeed, the whole of Jesus' life and ministry, suggests that our first investment should be in people. We are to invest ourselves in others; we are to use whatever resources we have in the service of others, whether that be material resources or personal resources of time, energy, training or talents. Jesus is the supreme example of someone who invested himself fully in others. He lived and died for others, for all of us. Saint Paul said of him that 'for your sakes he became poor so that by his poverty you might become rich.'

In today's parable, a crisis moment brought home to the steward that his true wealth consisted not in accumulating goods for himself but in establishing relationships within the community. It can take a crisis in our own lives to bring home to us that our true wealth lies in the loving relationships that we have formed with others, with our family, with our friends, and with those who cross our path in life, many of whom may live far from us and in very different circumstances to our own. The difficult and painful experiences in life can bring us closer to others and, thereby, to the Lord.

Twenty-Sixth Sunday in Ordinary Time
Being in communion

Am 6:1, 4-7; 1 Tm 6:11-16; Lk 16:19-31

We have tremendous opportunities for communicating with one another today, more than ever before in the history of humankind. I had an aunt who was a Dominican nun in South Africa most of her life. She died at the great age of ninety-seven. She sailed from Dublin in about the year 1917. During the eighty or so years my aunt was in South Africa she communicated with us by letter. She faithfully wrote to us in a very beautiful writing script, and she loved getting letters in return. The letter was her only connection with home for many, many years. As a result, her letters were always full of news, as were our letters to her. We don't write letters as much today because we have so many other ways of communicating. My sister has been living in Southern California for almost thirty years now and every week we speak on Skype. I am a recent convert to Twitter, partly on account of setting up a parish Twitter account. Twitter is a less personal way of communicating, but it is a very effective way of getting a short message to a large number of people. We have so many ways of communicating with each other today, regardless of distance.

Yet, in other ways perhaps we don't communicate as well with each other as we did in the past. The kind of neighbourliness that was part and parcel of life where I was growing up is not always in evidence to the same extent in these times. We hear reference to gated communities today. A gated community seems a little bit of a contradiction in terms. Gates are generally for keeping people out; they are hardly builders of true community. People seem to be more isolated today than they were in the past, especially those living alone. Yet, we all feel the need to communicate, to be with others, to connect with people. Many parishes have a good tradition of people gathering in various ways, forming communities of various types, in different settings. The schools generate a community among parents, as well as among the pupils who go there. The parish does likewise. There is a variety of groups in many parishes where people gather and connect in all kinds of good, healthy ways. There is a tradition within local parish communities of connecting with people in other communities who are less fortunate. Many young people go as volunteers to serve in different parts of the world for the summer.

The parable that Jesus speaks in today's Gospel is about a lack of communication between two individuals, a very poor man, named Lazarus, and an extremely wealthy man. The poor man had a great desire for a simple form of communication from the rich man; he longed to fill himself with scraps that fell from the rich man's table. The rich man had no desire to communicate with Lazarus. He couldn't but see him at his gate, but he took no notice of him; he was indifferent to him. His extreme wealth and comfortable existence isolated him from his fellow human being who was suffering under his nose. The rich man created a great gulf between himself and Lazarus, a gulf that endured into life after death. Although he was very wealthy, he was in reality very impoverished and it was in the life after death that the reality of the rich man's poverty became clear. He was now revealed to be the needy one, calling on Abraham to ask Lazarus to become his servant, bringing him water to quench his thirst. In the afterlife, the rich man was very concerned about the fate of his five brothers, but he had failed to recognise Lazarus as his brother during his earthly life. He failed to notice that God was calling out to him through Lazarus and that in responding to Lazarus he would have become genuinely rich, rich in spirit and in heart, rich in the sight of God. Not a great deal was being asked of the rich man. He was simply being asked to share a little of his abundance with Lazarus. That would have been a path to genuine riches for the rich man.

The parable reminds us that we are all very dependent on one another, and that is how God expects us to live. The Lord is constantly calling out to us in and through each other. We all have something that we can share and that others need. Apart from any material resources we may have (and many people don't have much to spare), we may have some time, some talent, some strength or insight. We each have some gift that the Lord is asking us to place at the disposal of others, and others have some gift that we need to receive and benefit from. Those who appear to have least to give us can have most to give us. We have all had the experience of sharing something of ourselves with someone only to discover that we ended up receiving from them far more than we gave them. This is the kind of human communication for which the parable asks us to strive. It suggests that this is the path to genuine riches, to fullness of life for all of us, here and now and in the hereafter.

Twenty-Seventh Sunday in Ordinary Time
A Gospel prayer

Hab 1:2–3, 2:2–4; 2 Tm 1:6–8, 13–14; Lk 17:5–10

There are a whole variety of ways in which we pray. Sometimes we pray in quite a formal way, as when we gather together for Mass. We pray aloud together, all of us using the same set of words. There are also times when we pray in a much more personal way, in a way that is unique to each one of us. Our personal prayer can take a whole variety of forms. It might be a very silent form of prayer during which we simply sit quietly in the Lord's presence; we become aware of his presence to us and we try to be present to him. At other times, we feel the need to say something, at least quietly to ourselves. During those times, we pray out of what is in our heart or on our mind; we bring our worries, our needs, our hopes, our joys before the Lord in a very personal way. We speak to the Lord out of what is most important to us, as a friend would speak to a friend. In that phrase of Cardinal Newman, 'Heart speaks to heart'. Sometimes when we allow our heart to speak to God's heart, we discover that our prayer is full of dark emotions. A very good example of such a prayer is the prayer of the prophet Habakkuk in today's first reading, 'How long, Lord, am I to cry for help while you will not listen; to cry, "Oppression" in your ear and you will not save?' Prayer has to be real. Indeed, that is the kind of prayer God wants from us.

There are times when, even when we are praying in this very personal way, the prayers that other people have composed can help us. Cardinal Newman has written some wonderful prayers. One of his prayers is, 'Lead, Kindly Light', which has been put to music: 'Lead, Kindly Light, amid the encircling gloom, lead thou me on. The night is dark, and I am far from home; lead thou me on.' It is a prayer we could pray when the way ahead seems unclear to us and we feel the need to turn to the Lord and ask for some light to enlighten us. In that way, Newman's prayer becomes our personal prayer; we pray it in our own way; we make it our own. Many people turn to favourite prayers of theirs because those prayers put words on what they experience within themselves.

Occasionally there are prayers which people pray in the Gospels that I find very easy to make my own. One example of such a prayer is the prayer of the disciples in today's Gospel reading, 'Increase our faith.' It is very similar to another prayer that we find in the Gospels on the lips of the father of a very sick boy, 'I believe, help my unbelief.' 'Increase our faith' is a simple yet profound prayer. If we pray at all, we have some faith. If we try to reach out to the Lord in some form of prayer, it shows that we have some relationship with the Lord, and what is faith only a relationship with the Lord that is marked by trust, love and hope. Yet, even though the fact that we pray is a sign of our faith, we can all pray the prayer, 'Lord, increase our faith'. The context of the disciples' prayer in today's Gospel reading was a challenging lesson from Jesus. He had just said to his disciples, 'If someone sins against you seven times a day, and turns back to you seven times and says "I repent", you must forgive.' Faced with this challenging call, the disciples cried out, 'Increase our faith'. Sometimes we do have a sense that the call of the Gospel is beyond us and that we are constantly falling short of where we feel called to be. Rather than get discouraged by that, we can simply pray, 'Lord, increase our faith'. Or, in other terms, 'Lord, deepen my relationship with you. Help me to respond more fully to your call. Empower me to become the person you want me to be.'

Our faith can seem very brittle at times. In the image of the prophet Isaiah that was quoted by Jesus in one of the Gospels, our faith can seem like a 'bruised reed' or a 'smouldering wick'. Our faith has taken a battering in recent years, certainly our faith in the Church, whatever about our faith in the Lord. So much in our culture today is hostile to our faith. The prayer 'Increase our faith' is a very contemporary prayer. It acknowledges that we have faith but that our faith is, at times, weak and vulnerable. The response of Jesus to the disciples' prayer in today's Gospel reading is striking, 'Were your faith the size of a mustard seed ...' It is as if Jesus is saying to his disciples, 'Even a little faith is something powerful. I can work powerfully in and through faith that is as small as a mustard seed.' I am reminded of Paul's statement in one of his letters that the Lord's power is made perfect in weakness. A little opening is all the Lord needs. Even though our faith seems weak at times, we should never devalue our little faith, because the Lord values it highly.

Twenty-Eighth Sunday in Ordinary Time
Thankful prayer

1 Kgs 5:14-17; 2 Tm 2:8-13; Lk 17:11-19

Our prayer can take a whole variety of forms. Yet, there is one form of prayer that is very common to all of us and that is the prayer of petition. It is a very valid form of prayer. In the Book of Psalms, the most frequent prayer is the prayer out of the depths of some distress, calling on God for help. We know of only one prayer that Jesus gave us to pray, the Lord's Prayer. That prayer is a prayer of petition, a communal prayer of petition; it has the language of 'we', 'us' and 'our'. Yet, that element of communal petition really only begins a few petitions into the prayer. The opening petitions do not have the language of 'we', 'us' and 'our', but rather the language of 'your', with the 'your' referring to God. In those opening petitions we are focusing not on ourselves but on God. We are asking that God's name be held holy, that God's kingdom come and that God's will be done. In the prayer of petition that Jesus gave us there is a very strong focus on God, especially in those opening three petitions.

There is another form of prayer that perhaps, does not come as naturally to us, where the focus is more on God than on ourselves, and that is the prayer of praise. It is closely linked to the prayer of thanksgiving. It is a form of prayer where the movement is very much away from ourselves towards God. It is a very selfless, God-centred form of prayer. We all learnt a very short prayer of praise when we were young, 'Glory be to the Father, and to the Son, and to the Holy Spirit, as it was in the beginning, is now, and ever shall be world without end. Amen.' A longer form of that prayer is to be found at the beginning of Mass, 'Glory to God in the highest'.

I have always found myself very drawn to the story that we find in today's Gospel reading. Ten lepers approach Jesus. They don't get too close to him because they are aware that they are required to keep their distance from those who don't have their disease. They stand some way off from Jesus but within his earshot because they have a communal prayer of petition, which they desperately want Jesus to hear and respond to, 'Jesus! Master! Take pity on us'. This is an example of the prayer out of the depths that is so plentiful in the Book of Psalms. You may be familiar with the prayer, Kyrie, Eleison, from the beginning of Mass, 'Lord, have mercy'. That is the prayer the lepers pray, 'eleison', 'have mercy'. We tend to think of 'mercy' only as 'forgiveness' but in the Gospels the quality of 'mercy' is any compassionate response to human need, whether that need is spiritual or, as in the case of the lepers, physical. Jesus responds to their prayer, but, not perhaps in the way they expected. Rather than healing them there and then, he tells them to do something; they are to go to the priests in the temple in Jerusalem whose role it was to officially declare whether or not a person who had suffered from leprosy was healed of it. The lepers trusted the word of Jesus and on the way to the temple they were cleansed. Sometimes our own prayers of petition are not answered in the immediate, direct way that we might have expected; we too have to trust that along the way we will experience an answer to our prayer.

Once healed, nine of the ten headed back to their communities and families, from which their disease had excluded them. Who could blame them? It was a very natural thing to do. However, one of the ten, a Samaritan, 'turned back' praising God at the top of his voice and when he reached Jesus he threw himself at Jesus' feet, thanking him. He alone recognised that in his healing he had been graced by God; he alone went beyond the gift to the Giver, to God, present and active in the person of Jesus. He saw his healing with different eyes to the other nine, with the eyes of faith, eyes that recognised God at work in his experience. In response to this one man's turning back, Jesus does not say, 'No one has come back to thank me except this foreigner', but, 'No one has come back to give praise to God, except this foreigner.' Jesus does not look for thanks for himself; he is completely God-centred, and so is this Samaritan, this religious outsider. It is because of his movement out of himself towards God in praise that Jesus says to him, 'Your faith has saved you.' He alone of the ten was truly a man of faith in God. This Samaritan encourages us to see all of life with the eyes of faith, recognising that the many good things that come our way in life have their source in God. He inspires us to respond to this recognition by praising and thanking God with all our heart.

Twenty-Ninth Sunday in Ordinary Time
Persevering faith

Ex 17:8-13; 2 Tm 3:14-4:2; Lk 18:1-8

We can all be prone to discouragement. We come up against various obstacles and over time we feel that they are wearing us down and taking energy away from us. Sometimes these obstacles take the form of other people who make life difficult for us for one reason or another. The result of getting discouraged can be to put less of ourselves into life. We can become half-hearted about everything. That temptation is understandable, but it is a temptation we need to keep on trying to resist.

The parable in today's Gospel reading puts before us a person who simply refused to get discouraged. The person in question is a widow who appears to be somewhat alone in the world. There is no mention of any children standing by her in her hour of need. Given that the average life expectancy of the time was about forty years of age, it is likely that the widow was relatively young by the standards of today. She certainly comes across as a very vigorous woman. She clearly believes that some great injustice has been done to her. She goes to the court looking for the justice that she is entitled to. Unfortunately, she finds herself having to deal with the worst kind of judge who neither fears God nor has any respect for others. This powerful man has no interest in the plight of this powerless woman. However, she refuses to get discouraged, even though a second injustice is being done to her by the judge who should have taken up her case. She keeps coming to him day after day until she wears down the judge's resistance. She exhausts the judge into justice. The powerless widow turns out to be very powerful after all and the powerful judge ends up cowering before the seemingly powerless widow.

The figure of the widow in that parable is a wonderful portrayal of the refusal to get discouraged, even when everything goes against you and you come up against the worst instincts of other people. Jesus paints this picture in words of a persevering widow who refuses to be discouraged because it captures the kind of faith that he is looking for from his disciples. Having spoken the parable, Jesus asks the question, 'When the Son of Man comes, will he find any faith on earth?' Jesus is asking, when he comes back at the end of time as the glorious Son of Man, will he find faith that has the same quality of dogged perseverance displayed by the widow. Jesus is calling for a faith that endures, that stays the course and refuses to give up, even when all the supports for faith seem to be taken away.

These have been difficult times for people of faith. A great deal has happened in our world, and particularly in our church, that has been a real challenge to faith. We have all experienced the temptation to discouragement. You hear people say that they are hanging on by their finger nails. Yet, Jesus seems to be saying in today's Gospel reading that to be a believer is to be a persistent believer. The supreme example of a persistent believer is Jesus himself. He remained faithful to the end, even to death on a cross. He was faithful to God, to the work that God gave him, which meant that he was faithful to those to whom God had sent him, all of humanity. Jesus refused to give up on humanity, even on the cross. If his life touched the lives of a few, he hoped that his death would touch the lives of many. His faithfulness overcame the darkness of sin, the sin that put him on the cross. Jesus' faithfulness revealed a God who does not give up on us, who does not easily get discouraged by our failures and resistances, who keeps faith with humanity. Pope Francis says that 'the power of God's love is able to overcome the darkness of evil'. In a similar way the power of the widow's persistence overcame the darkness of the evil that confronted her on every side. She showed a God-like perseverance and this is what Jesus calls for from his disciples.

In his letter to the Romans, Paul calls on the Church in Rome, 'Do not be overcome by evil but overcome evil with good.' The widow in the parable overcame evil with good. Jesus, on the cross, overcame evil with good. Jesus calls on us to have a faith that perseveres even in the face of evil. The Gospel reading suggests that such a persevering faith is made possible by prayer. The beginning of today's Gospel reading states that the parable of the persistent widow is about 'the need to pray continually and never lose heart'. Jesus suggests that he will find strong faith wherever there is strong prayer. We are more likely to have a persevering faith if we persevere in prayer. The example of the widow displays a persistent and courageous prayer in the face of evil. Such prayer opens us up to the Lord's strength and it is only in his strength that we can persevere in faith, even when the temptation to discouragement is strong. In the words of St Paul, 'I can do all things in him who gives me strength.'

Thirtieth Sunday in Ordinary Time
The prayer of the humble

Sir 35:12-14, 16-19; 2 Tm 4:4-8, 16-18; Lk 18:9-14

Prayer is something very personal to each one of us. How we pray can reveal a lot about ourselves and, in particular, about our relationship with God. This is especially the case with informal prayer. When we move away from the prayers that are set out for us, such as the communal prayers at Mass, and pray in our own words, we reveal how our heart is before God. There aren't that many contexts, at least within our own Roman Catholic tradition, where we give public expression to our own very personal prayer. Our informal prayer in our own words tends to remain private.

In today's Gospel reading, Jesus speaks a parable about two people who went up to the temple to pray. The setting in the temple is probably to be understood as a communal setting. There would have been other people present. In this communal setting these two men prayed aloud in a very personal way. They gave expression to what was in their heart before God. They lifted up their minds and hearts to God in the presence of other worshippers. The two men who went up to the temple to pray came from opposite ends of the religious spectrum. For the majority of Jesus' Jewish audience, the Pharisees would have been respected teachers. They not only taught others how to live according to God's law but they tried to live by God's law themselves. They took their faith very seriously and were highly regarded by the people. For a first-century Jew, a tax collector, in contrast, was an agent of Rome. Tax collectors purchased the right from the Roman authorities to collect taxes in a certain region. Whatever they collected over and above their contract was considered profit. It was presumed that they were corrupt and dishonest, likely to overcharge people. Many of them were wealthy at other people's expense. A tax collector would have been seen as a sinner, who likely had shown no mercy to others.

The prayer of the Pharisee begins well. He thanks God for his life lived according to God's law, thereby showing his dependence on God for all his good acts. This particular Pharisee has gone beyond what the Jewish law required. The law did not require that everything be tithed, but this Pharisee pays a tithe on all his possessions. There is also no requirement in the Jewish law to fast as often as twice a week, which this Pharisee does. He is being portrayed as something of a saint among Pharisees. He would have been seen as expressing outstanding piety; however, his prayer has one fatal flaw. In his prayer, he sat in judgement upon the great mass of humanity, conveniently represented in the temple by the tax collector. He expressed a mentality that any of us, especially those who take their faith seriously, can fall into from time to time. It is the mentality which compares our own virtuous actions favourably to those whose lives seem to us far less religious or spiritual. Paul in one of his letters very wisely declares, 'Do not pronounce judgement before the time, before the Lord comes, who will bring to light the things now hidden in darkness and will disclose the purposes of the heart.' The Pharisee has forgotten that obedience to God's law cannot be separated from loving one's neighbour as oneself. Good actions without compassion for others are not acceptable to God.

The tax collector stands far off from others, perhaps indicating his sense of isolation from the community. He does not even raise his eyes towards heaven, suggesting that he feels unworthy to be in conversation with God. In beating his breast, he acknowledges his sin. There is only one other place in Luke's Gospel where people make this gesture. The crowds who had gathered at Calvary to witness the crucifixion of Jesus, immediately after he dies return home beating their beasts. The tax collector's prayer is much more succinct than the prayer of the Pharisee. He recognises that he is a sinner who is in need of God's mercy. He has come to the temple believing that he can find forgiveness from God for his sin, and his humble prayer for mercy is without any judgement of others. Unlike the Pharisee, the tax collector is aware that he has nothing to offer God, but everything to receive from God. He knows that he can sink no further, and that if anyone is to rescue him, it can only be God. Whereas the Pharisee looked around comparing himself favourably to others, the tax collector looked within, comparing himself unfavourably to God. He recognises his own inner truth, such as it is, and he hopes, indeed he trusts, that God can take care of it.

Whose prayer found favour with God, the prayer of the religious professional or the prayer of the amateur? Jesus' own answer to that question would have probably shocked his listeners. It was the tax collector who 'went home again at rights with God', whereas the Pharisee did not. Of the two people who went up to the temple to pray, only one of them experienced God's hospitable love. The parable encourages us to place our trust in God, more than in ourselves. It assures us that if we come before God empty handed, recognising our poverty, God's loving mercy towards us will know no bounds.

Thirty-First Sunday in Ordinary Time
Seeking the Lord

Wis 11:22–12:2; 2 Th 1:11–2:2; Lk 19:1–10

Last Sunday the children who will make their first Holy Communion in May were enrolled as candidates for this sacrament at the family Mass. Before the children make their first Holy Communion, they will make their first Confession. The Gospel text that teachers use in preparing children for their first Confession is today's Gospel reading, the story of Zacchaeus.

The Zacchaeus story has a lot in common with the parable of the lost sheep, which the children are also introduced to in preparation for their first Confession. The shepherd who searches for the lost sheep is an image of Jesus who seeks out the lost. The shepherd seeks out the lost sheep and Jesus seeks out the lost Zacchaeus. Yet, the differences between the two passages are also obvious. The sheep in the parable takes no initiative; he simply waits until the shepherd finds him. The sheep is a rather passive figure. The same could certainly not be said of Zacchaeus. He doesn't wait around to be found by Jesus; he goes looking for Jesus. He is portrayed in the story as a very single-minded seeker. He really had to make an effort to see Jesus. Because he was a small man, the crowd blocked his view of Jesus. As a chief tax collector in the pay of the Romans, the crowd would have had a very negative opinion of him and would not have helped him to see Jesus. Yet, this man was a determined seeker; he overcame the obstacle of the crowd by climbing a sycamore tree to see Jesus. It was a rather undignified thing to do for a person of his position and it left him open to even more ridicule. He literally went out on limb to see Jesus, regardless of what others thought.

Zacchaeus is a much more interesting character than the sheep in the parable. He finds himself in a job which has brought him a lot of wealth, but he is clearly not satisfied. He is looking for something more, something deeper. His restlessness draws him to the person of Jesus. In today's second reading, St Paul prays that God, by his power, 'would fulfil all your desires for goodness'. I like that phrase, 'desires for goodness'. We all have such desires, the desire for what Paul calls in one of his other letters, 'Whatever is true, whatever is honourable, whatever is just, whatever is pure, whatever is pleasing, whatever is commendable.' These desires are deep in our hearts and they will surface in us every so often if we allow them to. Underlying all those desires for what is good, for goodness, is the desire for God, the source of all that is good, and the desire for Jesus, who is God-with-us, and who gives expression to all that is good. If we seek to be true to those desires for goodness that lie deep within us, we will be led to the Lord who alone can fully satisfy those desires.

When Zacchaeus went seeking Jesus in response to those deep desires within himself, he discovered that the Lord was already seeking him. All Zacchaeus wanted to do was see Jesus, which is why he climbed the tree. Jesus, however, wanted to do more than see Zacchaeus. He wanted to meet Zacchaeus, which is why he stopped under Zacchaeus' tree, called out to Zacchaeus by name and invited himself to Zacchaeus' home, 'Zacchaeus, come down. Hurry, I must stay at your house today.' The story of Zacchaeus encourages us to keep seeking the Lord, in spite of the obstacles that will be put in our way. It also reminds us that the Lord is always seeking us. Indeed, he seeks us even when we are not seeking him because, as he declares in today's Gospel reading, 'The Son of Man has come to seek out and save what was lost', and we are all lost to some degree.

Zacchaeus was far from perfect. He confessed to Jesus that he had cheated people; he had probably taken more tax from them than he was entitled to. Yet, the Lord sought him out. He sat at the table of this sinner, even though it scandalised the people of Jericho. The Lord's sharing the table of Zacchaeus freed him to repent, to change for the better. Jesus' presence to and respect for Zacchaeus brought to the surface his deepest and best desires. In the atmosphere of acceptance that Jesus created, Zacchaeus was enabled to set out on a new and better path. The Lord always meets us where we are. His loving presence to us empowers us to change for the better. As today's first reading declares, the Lord overlooks our sins, so that we can repent. Zacchaeus experienced the transforming power of God's love through Jesus. That same experience is open to each one of us. Zacchaeus had that one essential quality that opened him up to this experience of the Lord's love. It is a quality we all need. Like Zacchaeus, we are to keep seeking the Lord with all our heart, regardless of the obstacles we may have to overcome.

Thirty-Second Sunday in Ordinary Time
God of the living

2 Mac 7:1–2, 9–14; 2 Th 2:16–3:5; Lk 20:27–38

November is traditionally a month when we remember those who have died. We have all had to deal with death in one form or another. Many of us will have lost loved ones, sometimes in very tragic circumstances. The death of a loved one touches us in a way that no other experience does. Through this very personal and painful experience, we come face to face with the mystery of death. Many problems can be solved but the great mysteries of life often just have to be lived with, and death is one of those great mysteries. Whenever we encounter a problem of one kind or another, we can go to someone who has an expertise in that area to solve it. When we come up against the mysteries of life, such as death, it is our religious tradition that can be of most help to us. The great religious traditions of the world all engage in different ways with the great mysteries of life. They attempt to shed some light on the mystery of death in particular.

Within the same religious tradition, there can be different approaches to this mystery of death. In the time of Jesus there was more than one understanding of death within the Jewish tradition. One group, the Sadducees, did not believe in life after death in any real sense; they dismissed any notion of resurrection from the dead. In today's Gospel reading, they try to ridicule Jesus' belief in the resurrection of the dead, life beyond this earthly life. According to the Jewish law, if the husband of a woman died, his brother should marry her to ensure the preservation of his brother's line, so that the deceased brother lived on through his wife's children. The Sadducees put before Jesus the preposterous scenario of this situation repeating itself seven times, and, so, they wonder which of the seven brothers will the woman be wife to in the afterlife. Here was a scenario that was intended to stop the likes of Jesus in his tracks. To have one's religious beliefs ridiculed can be very disconcerting and unsettling; however, someone who was as rooted in God as Jesus was could not be so easily unsettled.

In his response to the Sadducees, Jesus declares that there is a radical difference between life in this world and life in what he calls 'the other world'. In this world we all die sooner or later. In the other world, Jesus says, people no longer die. Those who are judged worthy of this other world no longer need to live on through their children, which was the issue of the Sadducees; they themselves will live forever. Jesus does not spell out what life in this other world will look like; however, he does say that the children of the Resurrection will be sons and daughters of God. In other words, our primary relationship will be with God rather than with each other. We will be siblings of one heavenly father. Jesus' answer does not mean that deep human relationships based on love will not endure. In growing closer to God we grow closer to each other. As we are drawn into Jesus' own relationship with God, we become more fully the person God created us to be; our capacity to love is purified and perfected, and our loving relationships are brought to completion.

In response to the Sadducees' caricature of the life beyond this earthly life, Jesus is saying that life in the other world, what we call heaven, will be something so totally new that no earthly experience can compare with it. That is why St Paul in one of his letters declares that 'no eye has seen, nor ear heard, nor the human heart conceived, what God has prepared for those who love him'. Paul makes this statement even though he claimed to have seen the risen Lord and, in one of his letters, says that he was once 'caught up into Paradise'. He was obviously referring to some mystical experience. Perhaps he saw enough to realise that this other life was beyond seeing and hearing and conceiving and even beyond speaking about.

In the Gospel reading, Jesus goes on to speak of God as the God of the living. Even though Abraham, Isaac and Jacob have died, God remains their God; God remains alive to them and they remain alive to God. The bond of love and faithfulness that God has with these three great patriarchs has not been broken by death. Jesus implies that God's love for us, God's faithfulness to us, endures beyond this life. God continues to hold us in the embrace of his faithful love beyond death. Jesus believes in a God who keeps his promises to his faithful ones, even beyond this earthly life. All true human love is life-giving and God's love is supremely life-giving. God's love will bring new life out of our death. Even though Jesus does not describe this life in any detail, the most common image he uses for this life is the banquet. It is an image of communion which suggests that this heavenly life is one wherein all our deepest hungers and thirsts will finally be fully satisfied.

Thirty-Third Sunday in Ordinary Time
Endings and beginnings

Mal 3:19–20; 2 Th 3:7–12; Lk 21:5–19

We are coming towards the end of the liturgical year. Next Sunday is the last Sunday of the liturgical year and the following Sunday, the first Sunday of Advent, is the beginning of a new liturgical year. As the curtain comes down on this liturgical year, the Sunday readings highlight the reality of endings, of things coming to an end. The experience of 'endings' can be among the most painful and difficult of all our experiences. This is most obviously so when someone close to us dies. Even though our faith tells us that for them life has changed, not ended, and that, therefore, our relationship with them has changed, not ended, we are aware that the kind of relationship we have always had with them has come to an end. In November we remember our loved ones who have died, and who, we believe, are now sharing in God's eternal life.

The beginning of today's Gospel reading is about endings, not so much the ending of a human life, but the ending of a hugely significant institution. Jesus announces the ending of the temple in Jerusalem. This was a magnificent building of its time and was considered one of the wonders of the world. It dominated the city of Jerusalem; indeed, it could be said that it dominated the whole Jewish world of the time. Forty years after Jesus was crucified, in the year 70, that temple was destroyed by the Roman army in response to the Jewish revolt. The most significant institution of Judaism was no more; this was an experience of ending on a cataclysmic scale. Yet, Judaism survived. The leaders of Judaism at the time created something new out of the ashes of that revolt, while remaining in continuity with the past. It is often the way that when something that has been central to our lives, whether as individuals or as a community, comes crashing down around us, we find the strength and the wisdom from somewhere to keep going. Over time we can discover that the ending was also a beginning, that something grows from the great loss.

In the Gospel reading, Jesus not only announces the coming assault on the temple that would result in its destruction, but also the coming assault on his own community of believers. As he faced into his own passion, he foretold the passion of his followers. They would be persecuted and handed over to the political authorities; the members of their own families would betray them to these authorities; their way of life would generate great hatred from some. In a way, Jesus was referring to his disciples in every generation. He was talking about all of us. We may not have experienced persecutions on account of our relationship with the Lord; we may not have been disowned by members of our families because of our commitment to the values of the Gospel. Nonetheless, it is still the case that walking in 'the way of the Lord', can be as countercultural today as it was when Jesus lived and when the Gospels were first written. If we take that way seriously and try to live by it, especially in certain settings, it will cost us something. We may even stand to lose a great deal as a result. Our world, like the temple in Jerusalem, may come crashing down. Yet, the message of today's Gospel is that if we courageously witness to the Lord and his values, regardless of how that is received, we will not ultimately lose out. Jesus declares, rather, that our endurance, our faithful witness, will win us our lives. The endurance the Lord talks about is a graced endurance; it is not down to us alone; it is an endurance that he makes possible. He promises in that Gospel reading that he will give us the wisdom and eloquence we need to witness to him in an enduring way.

Such endurance – such faithful and courageous witness – may not express itself in grand deeds or striking gestures. It will more often mean doing the day-to-day things in the spirit of the Gospel, as the Lord would want them done. It will mean getting up in the morning and taking on the day with faith, hope and love. That is what Paul seems to be getting at in today's second reading. He is very bothered that some in the community are not doing the ordinary things well. They are 'doing no work themselves and interfering with everyone else's work'. Paul wants them to go on quietly working, using whatever gifts they have been given in the service of the Lord and others. This may sound somewhat prosaic; however, Paul was aware that the Gospel was witnessed to and lived out in our ordinary day-to-day living. It is in that context that we display the graced endurance Jesus speaks about in the Gospel reading.

Our Lord Jesus Christ, Universal King
The king and the criminal

2 Sm 5:1–3; Col 1:12–20; Lk 23:35–43

Of all the films I have seen in recent years, one that stays with me is entitled, *Of Gods and Men*. It is the story of a community of seven monks of the Trappist monastery of Our Lady of Atlas in Tibhirine, Algeria. They were murdered on 21 May 1996 by a radical faction of Islamic fundamentalists, much to the horror of the other Muslims in Tibhirine, whom they had been serving. The abbot of the monastery, Dom Christian, suspecting that such an attack could occur, had written his personal testament two years earlier to be opened only after his death. The closing words were addressed to the person who might be his killer, 'And you, too, my last-minute friend, who would not have known what you were doing. Yes, for you too I say this "Thank You" and this "Adieu" – to commend you to the God in whose face I see yours. And may we find each other, happy "good thieves" in Paradise, if it pleases God, the father of us both. Amen. Inshallah!'

Dom Christian was evidently a man who died as he had lived. He showed a profound respect for his fellow human beings, even for those who wished him harm and would eventually put him to death. There is a quality of mercy displayed in his testimony and in the life from which it springs that can only be of God. Dom Christian gives us a glimpse into the heart of God's merciful love, a love which embraces all of humanity. The human being that gave fullest expression to this merciful love of God was Jesus. Like Don Christian, Jesus died as he lived. In the verses immediately preceding our Gospel reading, Jesus prays to God his father for those who were responsible for his crucifixion. He recognised that their actions sprung from ignorance, 'Father, forgive them, for they do not know what they are doing.' Jesus had spent his life revealing God's mercy to the broken in body, mind and spirit. He died as he lived.

The person we often refer to as the 'good thief' had a very personal experience of the mercy of God on the hill of Calvary. This man was in no doubt about his guilt. 'We are paying for what we did.' He acknowledges his sin, and then entrusts himself to his dying companion. He may have committed a serious crime, but he had an insight into Jesus that the religious leaders who mocked Jesus as he hung from the cross lacked. He somehow recognised the truth in the mocking title over Jesus' head, 'This is the king of the Jews'. He understood that here indeed was a king, but a king whose kingdom was not of this world, and whose way of exercising his kingship was not of this world. Out of this great insight of faith came his intensely personal prayer, which believers have made their own down the generations, 'Jesus, remember me when you come into your kingdom'. It is a prayer for mercy, for a merciful remembrance. If Don Christian shows us how to give mercy, this man shows us how to ask for it. He is the last of a long line of people in the Gospels who cried out to Jesus, 'Have mercy on me.' Their prayer never went unheard, and this man's prayer would not go unheard either. Indeed, he received more than he prayed for. He asked only to be remembered. He was given the gift of companionship with Jesus in Paradise, 'Today you will be with me in Paradise.' Jesus had shared table with tax collectors and sinners in the course of his ministry. He would now share table with this self-professed sinner at the banquet of eternal life. The king and the criminal enter Paradise together.

Early Christian art often depicted the cross as a tree of life. These artists recognised that Jesus had transformed the cruellest instrument of death that the Roman empire could devise into a source of life, a font of grace, a wellspring of divine mercy and love. On the cross Jesus revealed his identity most fully as the face of God's mercy. He demonstrated a love that is stronger than sin, more powerful than death. Here is a quality of love that has inspired people like Don

Christian and so many others down the centuries. There was an outpouring of love and mercy on Calvary that has helped to make the world more civilised, more human, than it would otherwise be. The good thief had a very personal experience of God's mercy on Calvary. That same personal experience is open to each one of us. Like this good thief, we each can come before the crucified and now risen king in our brokenness and weakness, asking for a merciful remembrance. Our prayer too will be responded to in a way that goes far beyond what we ask for. Saint Paul says that every time we eat this bread and drink this cup we are proclaiming the Lord's death, the Lord's merciful love. In every Eucharist, the same Jesus who spoke to the good thief is present to us, offering us his companionship in our need. As recipients of the Lord's mercy, we are then sent from the Eucharist to show his mercy to others, in the spirit of the Trappist monk, Dom Christian.